At the Rumor of His Coming

At the Rumor of His Coming

✦

Looking to Jesus for Miracles and Healing

Henry L. Hudson

iUniverse, Inc.

New York Lincoln Shanghai

At the Rumor of His Coming
Looking to Jesus for Miracles and Healing

iUniverse books may be ordered through booksellers or by contacting:

iUniverse
2021 Pine Lake Road, Suite 100
Lincoln, NE 68512
www.iuniverse.com
1-800-Authors (1-800-288-4677)

UNPUBLISHED MANUSCRIPT

All scripture verses in this book come from the King James Version of the Bible.

There are ideas and opinions in this book that are contrary to the theology and doctrinal teaching of the Churches of God in Christ. My ideas and opinions are uniquely my own and are not a reflection of the teachings of the pastor of my church.

ISBN-13: 978-0-595-36680-4 (pbk)
ISBN-13: 978-0-595-81102-1 (ebk)
ISBN-10: 0-595-36680-5 (pbk)
ISBN-10: 0-595-81102-7 (ebk)

Printed in the United States of America

This book is dedicated to my wife, Zadie Hudson, and our daughters, Lakisha, Melissa, and Laverne. They are the anchors and strength of my life. This book is also dedicated to my family of orientation, which includes my father, Elder Albert Hudson, Sr., who died when I was almost four, as well as my mother, Marie Hudson, and my late grandmother, Charlotte Williams. They raised eight siblings and three grandchildren through hard labor, much prayer, and faith. I dedicate this book to my brothers and sisters, who were the source of my strength and whose love and care kept me through the dark nights of my soul. From the top: Odessa, Albert, Jr., Bernice, Betty, Jackie, John, and Richard. I owe you my life and my love forever. I owe debts of gratitude to Reverend Owen Rogers, Roosevelt White, and Calvin Parker, who became a part of the extended family by marriage. I dedicate this book to my sister-in-law, Sherann; and to the grandchildren with whom we grew up, Janice, Maxine, and Marvin. A special thanks to my first editors, Donnell Stewart and Ann Clausen; to Wendy Gray, my longtime colleague from work; to John Traynor, my spiritual brother and retreat partner; and to Ms. Rose, who are all my long-term friends. And finally, to my pastor, his wife, and all of my friends at the local church.

Contents

Introduction

Writing a book, like any public disclosure or sharing of ideas and beliefs, is a risky proposition. This is especially true if the subject matter is controversial. Politics and religion are two of the most controversial topics in American culture, and because this is a book about Jesus, healing, and religion, the potential reader will probably have many questions: Who is Henry Hudson? What are his credentials for speaking so confidentially and authoritatively about Jesus's gospel and God's true nature? What academic achievements, life experiences, and accomplishments would qualify him to lecture the world of modern Christianity about the role of healing in Jesus's ministry and its implications for the modern-day Christian church? By what right or authority does he suggest that perhaps the apostles, prophets, scribes, theologians, modern-day ministers, and teachers either missed the message of Jesus's basic gospel or misunderstood or misinterpreted his teachings?

These are important questions, and the answers will determine whether I will find audiences for these important ideas and issues. I have been encouraged by my editors at iUniverse to address the question of what qualifies me to write a book on Jesus's healing ministry and its relevance for the modern church. What they are suggesting is that I have to share with you, my potential readers and students, what there is about my life experiences that qualify me as an authority and teacher on miracles and healing in the Christian tradition. Because true knowledge is experiential—a synthesis of facts, information, and life experiences over time—I will share with you some things about my life as a Christian and my experiences with God, miracles, and healing.

There are several ways of acquiring knowledge. We can learn about things by observing what goes on in the world and through our experiences with these things. We can also acquire knowledge and information through examining the science, thoughts, and observations about our world and culture as they are recorded in books, records, and documents of various types. We also learn from the traditions that are passed down through the generations. Then there are the other things we come to know, things from inner sources that are sometimes defined as insight or inspiration. This inner source of information, synthesized as knowledge, is also identified as intuition, but I have found that its true name is Holy Spirit or the "Voice of God."

If I am to be your teacher, I must demonstrate the probable truth of what I am teaching and suggest ways of validating these truths. In this book, I will present some ideas and information relevant to my subject matter and identify the sources. Then I will share some personal experiences to show that God is continually blessing many of his children outside of our churches with unconditional miracles of healing. I am also suggesting that there are no consistent and reliable miracles of healing in most of our churches—something you will be able to verify from your own experiences. Finally, I will share with you my reasoning, based on scripture, as to why Christians, who are defined as followers of the Christ, are not doing the greater works in accordance with Jesus's words. Hopefully, I will be able to make some suggestions as to how we can begin to correct this great failing of the Christian church.

The veracity of my positions will be determined experientially. After reading this book, some pastors will establish specific healing ministries based on Jesus's teaching and the information in this book. As a result, miracles of healing will be manifested routinely in their churches. Others will continue to preach the old-time gospel. Souls will be saved and sinners will give their lives to Christ. *But the sick among the children of God in those churches will continue to suffer and die of the sicknesses and diseases that Jesus expected us to heal in his name.* What else could Jesus have possibly meant when he made the following statements? "He that believeth on me, the works I do shall he do also: and greater works than these shall he do; because I go unto my Father. And whatsoever ye shall ask in my name, that will I do, that the Father may be glorified in the son" (John 14:12-13).

I have had formal courses of study on the history of religion from an anthropological, sociological, theological, and historical perspective. I have also studied metaphysics and spirituality from a cross-cultural perspective. However, my knowledge of God and the fundamental ways in which God's will, works, and powers are manifested in the physical world is experiential, which means that I know some things to be true through my own experiences. I have learned who and what God is from my experiences of growing up in the segregated South in the 1930s with a widowed mother, seven siblings, two nieces, and one nephew. It was a household with one primary breadwinner. Thus, I experienced God in the sense that Abraham experienced him as Jehovah-jireh: "the Lord will provide"(Gen.22:14). My mother demonstrated that by the power of faith and prayer God will meet all of our needs. This experience gave me firsthand knowledge that God is not only a healer, but that he is also still in the miracle-working business. Our survival as a family was proof that God is real, and he provides for all of his children according to their needs.

First, let me share with you what I have learned about God through these experiences. I grew up in the small town of Waycross, located in the Bible Belt in south central Georgia. In an African American community of about five thousand, there were eight different mainline Protestant churches, including Baptist, African Methodist Episcopal (AME), three Pentecostal churches, a Catholic church, and the Jehovah's Witnesses Kingdom Hall.

My family included my father, mother, grandmother, two older brothers, three older sisters, two younger brothers, two nieces, and a nephew. My father was a pastor of one of the early Churches of God in Christ as well as a carpenter and brick mason. We were able to live a modest, lower middle-class existence because of the success of my father's home-building business. He built homes mainly for the people who could afford them: mostly Southern whites. He died suddenly in 1939 from gangrene that developed from an operation for ulcers. Prior to his death, my mother was a homemaker.

Immediately after his death, my mother went to work, as did my two older siblings, who were fifteen and seventeen. My eleven- and thirteen-year-old sisters were given the responsibility of taking care of the household and managing the younger children. As far back as I can remember, my mother was out of the house for most of the day working. She was a very good cook and an excellent seamstress. She usually had three jobs; she was a cook and nanny for the family of the local sheriff, a professional cook at the local hotel or restaurant, and making dresses for women. However, the combined income earned by her and the older children was barely enough to provide food, clothing, and shelter for the family. Financially, we were poor, but the household was rich in spirit. Education, work, family relationships, play, and religion were prized values in our home.

Although we grew up in a very fundamentalist, Pentecostal denomination, practical Christianity was the guiding force in my mother's life and in the family. It was a basic form of religious practice that reflected Jesus's teachings rather than the theologies and doctrines now forming the theoretical basis for modern Christianity.

Let me describe to you how God's love and power was manifested in our lives. My mother was a very strong Christian woman who accepted the responsibility for the life and well-being of eleven children. She had a powerful, living faith that God would provide whatever she needed to handle the task God assigned to her through the death of my father. She was in her early thirties when my father died: a beautiful young woman with a big responsibility. After we grew up, we often wondered why she never remarried. She shared with us that there were few men in those days willing to take on the burden of a large family. She also stated that she was not prepared to impose the authority and presence of a substitute father figure on her children. Her belief was that God would provide whatever was needed for the family to survive.

It is very difficult for me to imagine how she handled the stress of getting up before dawn every morning to walk over a mile to her first of three jobs, leaving the younger children in the care of the two older girls who were in their very early teens. I did not understand the source of her strength at that time. She would give them instructions for the day: making breakfast, dressing all of the younger children, taking the preschoolers to the babysitter, and getting everyone else off to school. What I do remember from this period of my life was that she went to church every Tuesday and Thursday night and all day on Sunday. I also remember that my mother prayed faithfully and continuously about all things, all the time.

There were many things she needed from God. She had to provide food, shelter, and clothing for eleven children. She also needed Divine protection, strength, and guidance to raise her children in an intensely hostile, racist culture that defined them as inferior and less than human simply because of their race. This culture was especially dangerous for young African American males. My mother, nevertheless, was quite successful in guiding us through the dangerous waters of this fundamentalist, white, Southern Christian culture.

Moreover, she taught us the basic Christian values of unconditional love, acceptance, and a nonjudgmental attitude. She also taught us to be kind and to practice forgiveness in the world at large. I have one vivid memory of how a true Christian handles adversities in the outside world. In the segregated South, almost every encounter between an African American and a white person was fraught with the potential for violence and humiliation. There were times when one of us would react to some hurtful encounter with a white person, as children will sometimes do, by saying, tearfully, "I hate white people." Mother would give a gentle hug, and say, "You cannot hate all white people because of something one person did to you. All white people are not mean and spiteful and besides, Jesus said we are supposed to love everyone—even people who do bad and hurtful things to us. You also have to forgive lest anger eat away at you and ultimately consume you."

What I am trying to say is that this humble, hardworking, informally educated woman was an ever-present witness to what it means to be a true follower of Christ. She was a woman of great faith who depended daily on God to supply her and her family's needs in all ways. Poor Southerners, both white and black, had no access to doctors and medical treatment except in the most severe cases. There were many things in the world that could suddenly kill you. Nevertheless, when one of us became seriously ill with anything or there was a medical emergency, I could hear my mother praying, "Come right now, Lord Jesus, because tomorrow may be too late. We need you right now." Without fail, the power of God's love, mercy, and grace would manifest in the household with miracles of healing or deliverance each and every time.

In fact, one of the names for Jesus in our household and in the larger African American community was "Doctor Jesus." We had very little access to doctors or hospitals in those days. Therefore, we had to depend on God for healing the many sicknesses and diseases common among poor people. Some, like polio, typhoid fever, lockjaw, influenza, and poisonous insect and snake bites, were quite common. They were very dangerous and killed many people. But through my mother's prayers and God's grace and miracles, we all survived.

My mother moved to New York City in 1948 for economic and educational reasons. One of my uncles owned a small restaurant in Harlem. He encouraged my mother to come to New York, offering her a job as the chief cook in the restaurant. He informed her that New York had an excellent university system that gave bright children from poor and working-class families an opportunity to earn a quality college degree. The most outstanding thing about the university system was that it was free. This opportunity provided solutions for several of the problems she had talked to God about for a long time. Foremost among them were greater economic opportunity for the family and the possibility of a college education for her children. By 1953, the four youngest sons had moved to New York City to be with her.

I graduated from high school in June 1954 with a Regent's diploma and a 3.5 GPA. This was good enough to get into the City College of New York (CCNY). In 1954, it was one of the elite colleges for the children of poor and working-class New Yorkers. Once I got there, I discovered that I was seriously handicapped by the very society that justified racial segregation and discrimination under the myth of the "separate but equal" doctrine. In my formative educational experience, I was an outstanding student in a highly flawed educational system. In addition, since I was thirteen, I had the burden of having to work full-time as well as go to school.

My first semester at CCNY was very traumatic. It was a highly competitive academic environment that did not provide any support for students with problems in specific subjects. We were told with some degree of pleasure during freshman orientation that CCNY had a 75 percent attrition rate. My background in math and sciences was dismal. Moreover, I had a full-time job working forty-eight hours per week in my uncle's restaurant. I could not keep up with the academic demands of the school and the economic necessity of having to work full time. I began failing academically for the first time.

It was a devastating experience. I was in a competitive academic environment with elite white students for the first time in my life and was unable to meet the challenge. Our culture taught us to take personal responsibility for whatever happened in our lives, so I took all of the blame for my failures. On some level, I concluded that society would view my failure as validation for the stereotypical myth of white superiority/black inferiority.

On another level, there was an intense anger directed at God and at white people in general. My anger at God was based on my limited perception that He really did not care about fairness and justice in this world. I thought he could not possibly love all of his children equally because white American Christians were permitted to "stack the deck" in their favor and blame African Americans for economic and academic failures. This anger toward God was based on my very limited understanding of how God operates in the physical world and in the life of humankind. I did not know at that time that "all things" truly work together for good.

I did not have sufficient experiences with life to know that spiritual (God's) law operates with the same force and certainty as physical law. I did not realize that every nation and individual was subject to the laws of reaping and sowing. It was difficult for me to see or understand at that time that God has a plan and a purpose for each of us. Be that as it may, I flunked out of CCNY after completing about sixty credits. I was drafted into the army and began to go through the motions of going on with my life. I also began the descent into alcoholism as a way of handling the complexities of my life and my inability to cope psychologically and spiritually.

To better understand what began to happen to me in my twenties, we have to go back to some of the consequences of my father's death when I was about four years old. The basic changes in our lives and in the family structure triggered a state of chronic anxiety, depression, and insomnia. When I was eight or nine years old, I remember feeling sad, frightened, and insecure. I never spoke with anyone about my feelings then because my mother had enough things to be worried about. Sunday evenings after church were my worst times—the world seemed to be a dark and gloomy place. The source of some of my problems was related to the fear-based religion practiced during those times.

Most of the sermons we heard in church were designed to create guilt for not being perfect and instilled a fear of dying and going to hell because of our sinful nature if we did not repent (seek the Holy Ghost and give our lives to Christ). I remember a sermon I heard when I was about seven or eight. The preacher said with fervor and conviction that "God sees everything you do and will punish you for your sin. He even knows your thoughts and will judge them. And if you are judged a sinner, you will certainly die and go to hell." When I heard this, I concluded that I was doomed. I had enough difficulties controlling my behavior as a child and had no control over my thoughts. So, at a very early age, I became fatalistic and resigned myself to the eternal flames of hell. I also remember having suicidal thoughts during this time.

I was a very bright and perceptive child. I believed that the adults around me were reliable and trustworthy, so I tended to take things adults said literally. In the Southern Christian culture, there was a lullaby sung to put children to sleep. Although I never remember my mother singing it, I knew the song:

> *Now I lay me down to sleep,*
> *I pray the Lord my soul to keep.*
> *If I should die before I wake,*
> *I pray the Lord my soul to take!*

The intended message was that God was watching over you while you slept, but you had to make sure and really pray for his protection. In case God failed to "keep" you and you died before you awaken, you prayed that you would go to heaven rather than hell! This song terrified me. The fear and uncertainty related to my father's death, my mother working most of my waking hours, and the fear of an angry and punitive God created tremendous fear and anxiety in my young life. This fear was reinforced by that lullaby and became an obsession with me. From about age six into my late twenties, I tossed and turned every night because I was fearful of going to sleep. Deep in my subconscious mind I held a fear of God and dying in my sleep! These childhood traumas led to my attempts to medicate the constant, intense emotional and spiritual pain during my early twenties.

I was painfully shy and self-conscious in any social setting. I had very low self-esteem and very little self-confidence. There was a perceptual disconnect between my objective level of functioning in the world—I had a moderate level of success in whatever I was required to do—and what I thought about myself. I was effective in my work and did well in all of my subjects at CCNY except math, science, and German. I was mannerly and well-behaved in public, even when I was intoxicated. Moreover, I was kind and polite with people and considerate of their needs and feelings. But I felt like an abject failure and a fraud.

Even though I had high moral standards and tried to live up to them, I felt guilty and morally corrupt in the sight of God. And because of my academic failure at CCNY, I felt I had failed my family and all of the teachers who nurtured me and expected such great achievement from me. Above all else, white Americans held the stereotypical view that African Americans were ignorant, dumb, and inferior to whites. Thus every African American, especially the brightest and most accomplished, carried the burden of having to serve as the "good example" for the white society. Subjectively, I saw myself as a failure who had "let down" the entire African American population.

It was unrealistic of me to expect that a bright African American student from a segregated colored school in the South would be able to enroll in an elite Northern college and succeed. The irony was that while the segregated school was inferior to the white schools, even the white schools in Georgia were not up to the standards of most of the New York City schools. Failure in that context was a certainty, especially if the student was also required to hold a full-time job and work forty-eight hours a week. Because I had never been challenged academically by the system prior to college and was able to consistently earn high grades with a minimal effort, I had no study discipline. Moreover, City College was highly competitive, and the institution was insensitive to the needs of potentially good students with particular handicaps. Therefore failure was preordained.

After two years struggling as a fully matriculated student with an average class load of sixteen credits per semester, I lost my matriculation and was transferred to the evening session. Evening session students usually held full-time jobs and attended school part-time. A group of us began to hang out in the local bars and clubs after classes. I made two very important discoveries during this time. First, alcohol took away much of my social anxiety and relieved some of my personal guilt, anger, and the associated emotional turmoil afflicting my life at that time. The second discovery was that I had to struggle all the time to keep my alcohol intake under control. Nevertheless, drinking became an essential element in my social life.

I struggled with work and college for two more years. In 1958 my deferment ended, and I was drafted into the U.S. Army in February of that year. Every young man entering the service is given a series of aptitude and placement tests. I scored high on all the tests, including the IQ test, and was given the opportunity to attend Officer Candidates School (OCS) once I completed basic and advanced infantry training. In 1958, the military was the first major American institution to end the discrimination and segregation that was practiced throughout the nation. However, the overwhelming majority of the officers and noncommissioned officers (NCOs) were white and racist.

In this racially charged environment, governed by the Universal Code of Military Justice, an African American soldier working for a career with the military was subject to unbearable pressures generated by a very hostile social environment. My mind was set on simply doing my two years of active duty and going back to New York. If I was not going to make the army my career, it did not make sense for me to go through the rigors of officer training. I'd rather take my chances in the civilian world. I understood the system very well. I did not want to subjugate myself to the stress of dealing with army life and the possibilities of war on top of realizing the full weight and absolute necessity of having to be a perfect soldier who had to be twice as good as any white soldier. All of this was not to gain rank but simply to avoid going to the stockade because of a mistake in dealing with a racist system. The slightest mistake in your social interactions could earn you a court-martial and a bad conduct discharge.

After five months of basic and advanced infantry training, I was assigned to duty at Schofield Barracks in Oahu, Hawaii. Although I was a very competent soldier and always held positions above my rank, I was never promoted above private first class (PFC) because of prejudice. I had a reputation among many white officers and NCOs of being an "uppity nigger" because I spoke proper English and did not behave in the stereotypical manner expected of African Americans. Another problem was that I probably had more formal education than most of my NCOs and other soldiers, and had very little difficulty learning anything the army had to teach. I was a good soldier, and the career army officers and NCOs could not understand why a bright African American male would pass up the opportunity to go to OCS and make the army a career. They concluded that I was antimilitary.

PFCs were paid about $99 per month, which meant that you could afford to buy a month's supply of cigarettes and go barhopping in Honolulu. I went on some momentous binges almost every month. I had my first memory blackout in Hawaii and progressed to middle-stage alcoholism by the time I was discharged from the service.

Following my return to civilian life in early 1961, I took the civil service exam for postal clerk and scored high on the test. I was hired a couple of months after passing the test. My life became an endless cycle of working and partying. I was working at the Church Street Station in Manhattan on the night shift (4:00 PM to 12:30 AM). We were paid every two weeks. A group of us would cash our checks in a bar across the street on Thursday night and begin a serious weekend of drinking and partying. Memory blackouts became more common, and I began to experience serious symptoms of chronic alcoholism (more frequent blackouts, morning shakes, and vague anxiety attacks or fears) along with intense guilt and remorse. I also began to think seriously about suicide.

I was going to doctors on average of two or three times a month. However, all of the tests and examinations suggested that most of the physical symptoms (chest pains, dizziness, chronic headaches, and stomach problems) were not related to an actual physical condition. I was prescribed a tranquilizer and sleep medication that did not alleviate my conditions. My general practitioner finally referred me to a psychiatrist who began psychotherapy and gave me stronger medications. These medications did not seem to help. Although I never took the medications if I was drinking, everything got worse. The emotional and spiritual pain grew more persistent and intense, and suicide seemed to be the only solution to my problems. The drinking binges became more frequent and the withdrawals more painful. During these painful withdrawals, I would often stand before the bedroom window in my tenth floor apartment, struggling against the impulse to jump.

During the early days of May 1965, I had planned to take a vacation. Although I did not know it at the time, it is common for alcoholics to conclude that the problems associated with a pathological lifestyle can be alleviated by leaving the physical and social environment and going to a different geographic location. In the AA Twelve Step program, this is called the "geographic cure for alcoholism." Under this illusion, I began to make plans to take a vacation to Europe. I was thinking that if I could just get away from the pressures of New York, my family, work, and friends for a short while, I would be able to get myself together. Unfortunately, I started a binge the first week in May. By the time all of my preparations were made and the vacation date arrived, I was trapped in a vicious cycle of drinking that I could not break.

A very short time after I started this binge, my consumption of alcohol quickly increased. By the second week in May, I was drinking over two and a half fifths of 100 proof bourbon every day just to ward off withdrawal symptoms, and drinking around the clock. My final binge, which lasted for about a month, was a horror beyond my ability to imagine or to describe. Every morning, I would stagger across Lenox Avenue at about 7:00 AM. When the bar opened for business at eight o'clock, I would go in and order four shots of liquor. Holding the shot glass with two hands, I would raise the first drink to my mouth. In quick succession, I would consume the other three shots. As the overwhelming "shakes and fears" slowly subsided, I would order another round and consume them. Then I would leave the bar, walk to the corner liquor store, and buy a fifth of alcohol. I would go back upstairs to my apartment and get ready for the activities of the day. Before midnight, I would buy another fifth of alcohol to get me through the night. By 6:00 AM it would be gone. Then the horror would begin all over again!

On June 3, 1965, I finally reached the end of my rope; I hit what is called my "psychological and spiritual bottom." I had the shakes and fears so bad that it took a half an hour for me to get the courage to walk across Lenox Avenue. At this hour of the morning, traffic is always light around 139th Street, but I had begun to "hear voices." The voices kept saying, "You are going to die. You are going to die." The voices subsided once I took my medicine (alcohol). By three o'clock that day, I realized that if something dramatic did not happen, I would not survive another night. I knew I would be compelled to jump. Sitting on the bar stool in this desperate state, I began to pray. I said, "God, I cannot live like this. I must have help." Immediately, a voice (the Holy Spirit) spoke in my mind and said, "Call Alcoholics Anonymous."

I had no knowledge of Alcoholics Anonymous (AA), what it did, or how it did it. But I walked out of the bar, found the number in the telephone book, and made contact. The person who spoke to me asked some questions about who I was and whether I thought I had a drinking problem. I answered the questions and was told to go home, that someone would visit me and help with the problem. I did not think that I could safely wait in my apartment for someone to come, so I asked for the address of the AA Intergroup office. I took a cab down to First Avenue and Thirty-first Street in Manhattan. There I found the beginning of my salvation and began the process of experiencing a profound gift of emotional, spiritual, and physical healing. It was as powerful and real as any of the miracles performed by Jesus.

Depression is an acute sickness of the soul. It is characterized by chronic feelings of powerlessness, hopelessness, meaninglessness, and emptiness. Depression is also marked by social isolation and feelings of being separate and different from other human beings. It is a deadly sickness of the human spirit that overwhelms all other realities. For example, ordinary people who are otherwise healthy and successful, and held in high esteem by their families and friends, die from this disease. They kill themselves because the spiritual pain is so intense and the feelings of powerlessness and hopelessness are so overwhelming.

This condition affects a significant percentage of Americans of all ages, gender, race, creed, and color each year; it is not limited by social status, wealth, or fame. As a matter of fact, I read an article in the *New York Times* a few years ago that the manufacturers of Prozac, Paxil, and Zoloft—the three most frequently prescribed antidepressants—had gross sales of over $7 billion a year. Medications treat symptoms, of course, but the healing of a depressive neurosis is a difficult and complex process.

My addiction to alcohol and tranquilizers was an attempt to medicate symptoms which ultimately failed. When I cried out to the Lord in distress, as David must have done, he heard my cry. Strangely enough, God did not direct me to the church of my youth, which was about ten blocks from my house. During this period of time, I went to church many times to receive prayers for healing. I believe that had the Holy Spirit instructed me to go to church, throw myself on the altar, and be saved, I would have done that.

I know that I would have been able to give up alcohol and drugs and could have acquired a measure of healing if "I was saved and sanctified" or made a commitment to accept Christ in my life as Lord and Savior, and lived according to the theology and doctrine of this Pentecostal church. God, however, had another plan for my life. He directed me to AA rather than to my church because it was through the AA experience of healing and recovery that God would prepare me for my life work as a therapist, healer, miracle-worker, and teacher.

The fellowship of AA worked for me and for millions of other sick and suffering people because it is one of the most important and powerful paths of spiritual and emotional healing that God has given humanity. AA is the "miracle drug" for the treatment and healing of a most complex mental and spiritual illness. At the heart of every spiritual sickness, including what theology defines as sin, is the belief that somehow you have become alienated or separated from God. What I discovered immediately in my AA experience was that no matter what I felt or believed, *God was never far from me.*

On the walls of every room where AA meetings are held are postings with fundamental information about God. First and foremost is the message that God is the God of all people who hears the prayers of all of his children—the good and the evil, the saved and unsaved. In the Twelve Steps program, I learned that God answers prayer, and that he could and would restore me to "sanity." There were reliable witnesses in the AA rooms throughout New York City who testified daily to this truth. I learned that God was an unconditionally loving father, and I could receive whatever I needed from him simply by asking.

You must remember that according to my religious upbringing (the Church doctrine I learned), I was a sinner who would die and go to hell if I did not repent. The theology of this religious denomination then provides a definition and context to what it means to repent. But I repented in the sense that Jesus used the word: I changed my ways of thinking based on new information and began to walk a different life path. I went to meetings regularly. Whatever AA activity was recommended to me, I was willing to do it.

Low self-esteem and acute self-consciousness were major factors in my academic failures. In college, I could not even make an oral recitation. But I learned how to express myself verbally in AA through the process of sharing at meetings and speaking in public when I served on the AA Inter-group Office's Public Education and Information Committee. Above all else, I prayed daily for strength and guidance to get past my anxieties and learned how to work my way through depression. After about a year in AA, I had learned how to "let go and let God." I could fall asleep at night (insomnia healed!) without medications. Slowly but surely, on a day-by-day basis, I embarked on this journey of healing that has brought me to the place where I am today in the world and in God.

I have worked in the field of substance abuse and employee assistance programs since I graduated from college (I returned to college during my second year of recovery and graduated in 1970). I worked as a counselor and as an assistant program director of a comprehensive, hospital-based treatment program. I also worked for three years as a program analyst for the New York City Bureau of Alcoholism Services. In 1975, I was recruited by a large prestigious Medical Center in New York City to develop and implement one of the world's first hospital-based employee alcoholism programs.

One of the things I have learned in my professional career in the substance abuse and mental health field is that healing sickness and disease is more important to God than religious proselytizing. I believe this because of what Jesus taught us about the importance of healing in his gospel and because of my life experiences since I came into recovery in 1965. My recovery was a part of the experiential healing path chosen by God to train and prepare me for my life assignment as a spiritual teacher, therapist, and healer.

I have been employed as the director of a hospital-based employee assistance program (EAP) for the past thirty years. I was initially hired as a substance abuse specialist, which was a new treatment specialty in the 1970s. However, at that time, there was no academic course of study leading to a degree in alcoholism or substance abuse counseling, so the majority of practitioners were individuals in recovery with some type of college degree.

At this hospital, I worked under the general supervision of the medical director of the occupational health services (OHS). When the program was first implemented, the medical staff at OHS had a list of sixty employees diagnosed with alcoholism. A number of these employees had other psychiatric diagnoses. This program evolved out of the need for a reliable, effective treatment resource for working-class employees. I began to treat this population with a degree of success (80 percent recovery rate).

One day, the medical staff referred an employee to me after she had come for a referral to the plastic surgery clinic. She was a frequent visitor to health services with a wide variety of vague symptoms. She believed that her face was disfigured, although no one seemed to understand what she was talking about. The OHS nurse suggested that they refer her to me for what I believed was an evaluation. At the conclusion of the evaluation, I informed them that the employee was paranoid and needed to see a psychiatrist. I was told that they had referred her to psychiatry many times, but she did not seem to be getting any help. The medical staff referred her to me out of desperation. The nurse said to me, very sweetly, "We know that she has a psychiatric problem, but we think that you will be able to help her."

In the assessment it was revealed that this employee had a long psychiatric history, including a hospitalization in a state psychiatric facility when she was eighteen. She had a psychotic episode in a bank when she imagined that the walls in the bank were covered with eyes that were staring at her mockingly. She had difficulties in public because she believed that people were staring at her imagined facial disfigurement. This employee was in therapy with me for over ten years and eventually recovered from her condition. She was the first employee referred to EAP for psychiatric reasons. Today about 85 percent of our cases are for problems other than substance abuse, with a vast majority being treated for anxiety and depression.

The EAP is essentially the mental health clinic for the hospital's employee population. We get referrals from every segment of the employee population. Our caseload includes doctors, administrators, nurses, technicians, and service workers. If you know anything about a medical center, you know that everyone involved in direct treatment or patient care has a degree or certification that validates they have been properly trained and are qualified to provide the service. Furthermore, every direct-care provider receives direct supervision. *I am the only mental health provider in the medical center with no formal credentials and no direct supervision of my day-to-day clinical work.*

Nevertheless, my staff and I have earned the respect and trust of the medical staff, hospital administration, union leadership, and general employee population by the quality of our work. Thousands of employees have been successfully treated for a wide range of problems, including serious psychological problems. They have come to us as self-referrals or have been sent to us because their job is in jeopardy. Many of our successes are viewed in the work setting as "miracles of healing." My success as a therapist and healer is directly attributed to God's divine guidance. His guidance placed me on an experiential spiritual path of individual healing. I have had work experience at several different types of substance abuse programs and that has prepared me to do the work of therapy and healing that I am currently doing.

Sometimes a client will ask me about my credentials or academic training as a therapist. They ask the question because there is nothing hanging on the walls of my office that will validate my qualification to do therapy. I will simply assure them that academically, I am a sociologist. But I will tell them that I am a therapist and a healer, who experientially may be one of the best therapists in the medical center. I do not brag because it would seem presumptuous, but what I am saying is that I am trained by the Holy Spirit, in the Jesus School of Miracles and Healing. The healing power found in this school is so effective, that there is nothing that a client can bring that cannot be healed.

Moreover, no matter how severe the emotional or spiritual conditions that have brought them to my office, I can assure them that there is a solution. Our service is a place with a reputation for healing in the hospital community. We have never had to market our services within the medical center. There are no posters in the office corridors or brochures on desks and tables saying, "This is your EAP. If you have problems with this, that, or the other, please contact us. We will help you." Over 80 percent of our caseload is a word-of-mouth referral, where a friend or coworker will recognize that an individual is having a problem and will suggest, "You should call Mr. Hudson or Ms. Wendy Grey at Staff Counseling. They will help you!" Within the medical center we have the reputation as a modern-day Gilead—a place where miracles of healing are the rule rather than the exception.

Thus, they can be assured that they will get the help they need, and it will not be long in coming. If it is a problem or situation I am familiar with then I will begin the work. If it is something new or I come to a place where I do not have the answer, my prayer is, "Lord what am I supposed to do or say now?" God has never failed to give me the words to say or the instructions about what I should do. In thirty years of practice, we have had many employees coming to us in either a suicidal or homicidal emotional state. By the grace of God, we have never had a client walk away from our office and act on those inclinations.

As the awareness of my spiritual gifts and abilities to heal evolved and manifested themselves in both my recovery and my work life, God began to reveal and suggest that he had a larger plan for me. My first conscious efforts as a healer of physical sickness and disease occurred in the late 1970s, shortly after I came into

AA. I had a small mole on my left arm that began to grow and cause me pain. In the American culture, we are taught that if a skin mole should grow or change, you should have it examined by a doctor because it may be malignant. So I went to my doctor, who examined my arm and declared that I should not worry about the mole. The implication was that it was simply a skin mole and was not malignant. But being the hypochondriac that I was at that time, I did worry. One night I was directed by the Holy Spirit to pray for the mole rather than worry about it. I laid hands on the arm over the mole, prayed, and in a very dramatic fashion, it withered and fell off in a couple of days. I still have a small brown circular scar on my left arm where this mole used to be.

In early 1980, I met my best friend, soul brother, and partner in the work of spiritual teaching and healing. John T. was in recovery and worked as a counselor in a large utility's substance abuse program. We met when we worked with Bronx AA members to establish an AA group at the medical enter where I worked that could accept and welcome addicts who were also addicted to "hard" drugs. This was before Narcotics Anonymous (NA) was developed. Drug addicts or people addicted to both alcohol and drugs were not permitted by the guide book of the AA Fellowship called the *Twelve Traditions* to openly attend AA meetings and use the Twelve Step recovery program. They could attend AA meetings but were not permitted to talk about their active drug addiction.

John, who had a dual addiction, became very active in Narcotics Anonymous. Through his contacts and work with one of the oldest successful twelve step oriented inpatient treatment and rehabilitation programs, he was approached by a priest whose order was sponsoring a spiritual retreat for men and women in the NA fellowships and was asked to serve as a co-facilitator. After the second year of working with this very difficult group—difficult from a traditional religious point of view—the priest suffered from burnout. John assumed the responsibility of facilitating the spiritual retreat for NA men the following summer and for the female NA in a separate women's retreat. Having the full responsibility for a retreat for over one hundred men and women in different stages of recovery proved to be a greater burden than one person could bear.

John came by my office one morning in April 1983. I had not seen him in a while, and as we talked about what had been going in our lives over the past couple of years, he told me about his experiences with the NA retreats. John then asked me if I would help him facilitate his next retreat. My response to him was that I did not know anything about spiritual retreats. He told me, "You are one of the most spiritual people I have ever met—you will do fine!" Thus, my "career" as a spiritual teacher and healer began. It was the beginning of a more public and formal teaching and healing career as I describe in greater detail later in this book.

In these retreats, our themes always come from God through the medium of prayer and meditation. We share stories with the participants about the many miracles of healing we have witnessed in the Twelve Step rooms. We would always tell them about God's unconditional love for all of his children. We shared that they had a right, as children of God, to simply ask for whatever they needed from the Father. We told them to not doubt and they will have it. We reminded them that Jesus taught us this and shared that God has demonstrated this truth in the AA and NA rooms.

In my lectures to the group, I would always talk about the miracles of physical and spiritual healing I witnessed in my recovery and experiences. After my presentation, some of those in attendance would speak with me during the breaks, stop by my room and request a prayer or healing for a disease they were suffering with, or ask for a prayer for a loved one. By our faith, many miracles of healing were given by God. By faith, many conditions were healed—conditions that had persisted for years despite medical efforts at treatment. After a couple of years, we added a healing workshop to the curriculum, and God always revealed his presence through miracles of healing.

During this time, I was not a member of any church. My ministry of teaching and healing was manifested in my work in the secular world and in my recovery activities. My wife, who grew up in the African Methodist Episcopal church, joined my mother's church, a local COGIC, after we were married in 1973. I did not feel a need to be involved with formal religion or church life at this time. However, after my children were born, I knew that it was important for them to be in a church, especially during their formative years. My belief is that there is no organization within society playing a more important role than church in the development of spiritual and moral values. I was quite confident that I could neutralize the negative effects of traditional religious beliefs on my children and correct much of the deeply embedded misinformation and contradictions about God contained in the majority of current Christian theology and doctrine.

It would have been hypocritical of me to insist that my children go to church regularly if I was unwilling to go. I did not believe then nor do I believe now that church membership and the rituals of holiness are more important to God than how we behave and treat one another. In fact, Jesus did not give us any instructions about the essentialness of religious rituals and ceremony. But he did say that it was important that we love one another as he had loved us!

I joined the church in 1985 specifically to develop a counseling service in the church for both members and the community. I believed that God wanted me to be there because I had two gifts to share. The level of my skills is such that a major medical center pays me a salary plus benefits valued at almost $100,000 annually. I also had demonstrated the ability to inspire miracles of healing. These skills and services have been available for free to church members, some of whom have past histories of substance abuse and are not in a twelve-step recovery program. In the twenty years I've been at the church, I have averaged about two clients a year. Moreover, there has not been any interest so far in my gifts as a healer.

Before I became a regular church member and a deacon, I had a healing ministry in the secular world. I was able to instill faith and negate doubt and unbelief in the minds of men and women who were not religious or did not belong to any church. They may have grown up in a religion, but by the standards of their original church, they are out of fellowship; in the language of Pentecostals, backsliders, or unrepentant sinners who we believe are destined to die and go to hell if they do not repent. This is the question: *if I am able to inspire a sufficient amount of faith and neutralize enough doubt that miracles are possible among nonbelievers, should not a pastor, minister, or Christian teacher be able to do the same in a congregation of believers?*

The recovering alcoholics and addicts who have been attending our annual retreats and the healing workshops for over twenty years have received and witnessed more dramatic miracles of healing than the members of an average church congregation. It appears to me they are the same mix of ordinary people who flocked to Jesus for healing. Since I have been a member of my church, I have debated within myself about the possibilities of developing a healing ministry in our church as a model.

In this book I will examine an issue which has troubled me for over twenty years. The issue is related to the fact that Jesus clearly said that any of his followers, including every modern-day Christian, should be able to consistently heal any sickness. There is no reliable healing in the modern-day Christian church and that has puzzled me. I do not know of any individual Christian or church where I can send someone I know with cancer or AIDS and have a degree of certainty that they will be healed. However, if I were living in Jesus's day, I could have confidently sent them to Jesus, to one of the seventy (Luke 10:17), or to the unnamed healer (Mark 9:38) and they would be healed. I believe a fresh examination of the scriptures will give us the answer to why there is little or no healing in the modern church.

The question has been whether God placed me in this congregation so that these gifts could be used to manifest the power of God in the form of miracles of healing. Moved by the Holy Spirit, I decided to develop a proposal for a healing ministry that I believe would greatly enhance the ministry. One of the objectives of this book is to explore the possibilities of developing a viable healing ministry in the modern-day Christian church, and to provide some instruction and scriptural justifications for integrating healing into our Christian ministries.

Writing this book is an act of casting my religious fate to the wind. I do not know if there is an audience for what I have to say or a willingness to recognize that I am not the originator of the information contained here. Nevertheless, this book is my commitment to Jesus, my teacher and my guide, and to my Father to do this work. If there is no place within the structure of organized religion for healing, then I will do this ministry in the secular world. Then again, I would be following the Master's healing tradition. Very few of his miracles were performed in the synagogues; the vast majority of Jesus's miracles of healing were done in the world.

1

Sickness and Healing

The majority of Americans are fearful of sickness and disease. By many different means, we try to protect ourselves and our families from these threats. We look to the medical profession and science for information and direction to protect ourselves from these threats. As a matter of fact, health insurance and medical services consume a significant part of a family's budget. For example, a recent article from the National Coalition on Health Care reports that Americans spent approximately $1.8 trillion on health care in 2004. This is four times the amount that the U.S. government spent on national defense. It was noted in the report that 45 million Americans are uninsured. What this means is that millions of American families, many of whom are Christians, are just one major sickness away from total financial ruin.

Because serious illnesses often lead to suffering and death, many Christians live in constant fear of being sick or of contracting a dreaded disease and dying. These fears and concerns are compounded because should you or a family member go to a citadel of healing (a hospital or medical center) for treatment, more bad things may happen. *New York Times* journalist Steven J. Spears quoted a health care expert who said, "Today, going into an American hospital seems about as safe as parachuting off a bridge. An estimated ninety-eight thousand Americans die each year as a result of medical error, and an equal number succumb to infections they acquire in a hospital" *(New York Times*, August 30, 2005).

Another recent article in the *New York Times* by the journalist David Leonhardt highlighted another problem in that "studies of autopsies have showed that doctors seriously misdiagnose fatal illnesses about 20 percent of the times. So millions of patients are being treated for the wrong disease (*New York Times*, February 22, 2006). Furthermore, millions of Americans, including many Christians, die each year from diseases that science cannot cure. Yet we continue to invest our hopes and resources in medicine, while ignoring another potential source of healing in which we have little faith.

In the Gospel of Matthew, there is this report: "And Jesus went about all Galilee, teaching in their synagogues, and preaching the gospel of the kingdom, and healing all manner of sickness and all manner of disease among the people. And his fame went throughout all Syria, and they brought unto him all sick people that were taken with divers diseases and torments, and those which were possessed with devils, and those which were lunatic, and those that had the palsy; and he healed them" (Matt. 4:23–24).

Although we are blessed with the greatest number of superbly trained health care professionals and the most advanced health care institutions in the world, there are many conditions they are able to treat but cannot heal. We also spend tremendous amounts of money on health care and medications. Nevertheless, millions of people continue to live in fear of diseases like cancer, AIDS, diabetes, and heart attacks. However, the people of Jesus's day did not have to worry about these things the same way we do! Their only concerns were when will Jesus the great physician be visiting the area, and how can I make sure that I am there at the appointed time? Or if Jesus could not get to their particular town or village, they may wonder when one of the seventy or the unnamed healer we are told about in Mark would arrive. Given the records we have in the Bible and the instructions we have from Jesus, why is there no evidence of consistent miracles of healing in our churches?

I am a social scientist and a practicing born-again Christian. After I returned to the church in the mideighties, I read the entire Bible for the first time. I did not follow any of the Bible study plans that are so prevalent in Christianity, but I read it as I would read a textbook. When I first read the fourteenth chapter of John, I was absolutely stunned. I believe that Jesus said, quite plainly, "He that believeth on me, the works that I do shall he do also; and greater works than these shall he do; because I go unto my Father" (John 14:12). The reality is that the greater works of healing are not being done in the Christian church. We are doing many other things that may be pleasing to God, but we are not doing consistent healing.

Maybe we are not doing the greater works of consistent miracles of healing because we don't know how to do them. Or maybe it is because we believe that to "bring sinners to Christ" is our first priority. However, there is specific information concerning our obligations to do miracles of healing in the reports we have of Jesus's life and his teachings. To duplicate his works, we must have the willingness to search for the information Jesus gave us about healing, believe in it, and then use it.

According to the Gospel of Mark, Jesus's public ministry began shortly after he was baptized by John the Baptist. After being driven by the Spirit into the wilderness for forty days and tempted by Satan, "Jesus came to Galilee preaching the gospel of the kingdom of God, and saying, 'The time is fulfilled, and the kingdom of God is at hand: repent ye, and believe the gospel'" (Mark 1:14–15).

Jesus then called his disciples and began his ministry of teaching and healing. In the teaching aspects of his ministry, he taught some fundamental truths about himself and about the true nature of God. At the same time, he began to demonstrate the validity of these truths through an intense ministry of healing and by performing many miracles. Jesus's life and ministry were the embodiment of the "good tidings" he was bringing to the world. The basic message of Jesus's gospel was that God had truly manifested in the physical world in a direct and profound way. Furthermore, in the person of Jesus, God made it possible for humanity to know his true nature and understand God's overall purpose for our lives.

Mark reports that in the very beginning of his ministry, Jesus went into Capernaum and began to teach a new and astonishing doctrine. In the synagogue where he went to teach, Jesus did something that was even more astonishing to the people who were there. A member of the congregation was plagued by what was believed to be a demonic spirit that tormented him with loud voices, "And Jesus rebuked him, saying, 'Hold thy peace, and come out of him.' And when the unclean spirit had torn him, and cried with a loud voice, he came out of him. And they were all amazed, insomuch that they questioned among themselves, saying, 'What thing is this? What new doctrine is this? For with authority commandeth he even the unclean spirits, and they do obey him'" (Mark 1:25–27).

From the earliest stages of Jesus's ministry, it was apparent that healing was an essential element of the "good news" he was bringing into the world. At a later point in his ministry, Jesus instructed the seventy men he sent on a healing mission to "heal the sick that are therein, and say unto them, 'the kingdom of God is come nigh unto you'" (Luke 10:9).

It was very quickly established that a healer greater than Moses, Elisha, or any of the prophets had come into the world in the person of Jesus. According to what Jesus said, a miracle of healing was a sure sign that the kingdom of God, which can be defined as the place where God is always present, was brought close enough that its power could be manifested in a direct way in the material world. As a result, everyone present at the time of the healing was able to immediately see and experience the consequences of the miracle; in the experience all could know that God had come nigh unto them in a very special way. Anyone who saw the miracle would never forget it and were forever changed by the experience of Jesus's miracles and his powerful acts of healing.

The miracles of healing which Jesus did were probably as much of an attraction for the multitudes drawn to him as his basic message about God and the kingdom of heaven. Health problems were surely of great concern for people in Jesus's time, just as they are today. Thus, it is quite instructive for us to realize that the issues of sickness and disease in the lives of ordinary people were addressed in the initial stages of Jesus's ministry. Healing was an important component of almost all of his major interactions with the people of his day.

The scriptures clearly reveal Jesus's miracles of healing were a powerful attraction, causing great multitudes to assemble at the rumor of his coming. It is certain that if a healer with the power and status of Jesus, the unnamed healer found in the Gospel of Mark (9:38), or one of the seventy mentioned by Luke (10:17) could be found in any church in America today, anyone afflicted with cancer, AIDS, schizophrenia, or any of the other incurable conditions that afflict humanity would flock to that church and be healed. In the process, the power of God would be manifest with such force and clarity that the reality of God would be difficult for the world to ignore.

While sickness and diseases are still major problems for church members and their families, healing has not been given the same degree of importance in the modern church as Jesus gave it. I have not heard of a church that has a specific ministry of healing as an integral part of its organizational structure. I believe that the major obstacles to consistent miracles of healing in the church are related to the doubt that is created in the minds of Christians by the many contradictions about the true nature of God which are structural elements in our theologies and doctrines. Thus, it will be very difficult for Christians to learn the principles of healing that Jesus demonstrated in his teachings unless we develop a more consistent theology and doctrine based exclusively on what Jesus taught about God's true nature and his relationship with all human beings; and about the prerequisites or necessary conditions for healing to be accomplished.

It is essential that we remember that Jesus's miracles of healing were as important in bringing us into the knowledge of God and his kingdom as any theology or doctrine we are currently teaching in our ministries. In the gospel of Jesus Christ, there are clear and specific instructions about healing that can be learned and taught. And finally, Jesus's specific charge to us was that we shall do the works that he did: mainly, healing the sick, performing miracles, and manifesting the love of God in our lives and through our Christian behavior.

It should be quite apparent that healing was a major focus of Jesus's ministry. Hence, according to scripture, Jesus's miracles of healing were as important to God's overall message to the world as the verbal content of Jesus's gospel. Therefore, I contend that one of Jesus's purposes in coming into the world was to teach us the true nature of God and his purpose for our lives. One of God's purposes for our lives, according to Jesus is to learn to do the things Jesus did, including healing all manners of sicknesses and diseases.

I will now introduce the idea, for discussion and consideration, that much of Jesus's basic teachings were misinterpreted and misunderstood by the disciples. As a result, the ensuing doctrine forming the theological basis for modern Christianity is based more on the Old Testament version of God and the laws of Moses than on what Jesus taught about God and his true nature. Consequently, the modern-day church is failing in its mission, as Jesus stated it, to manifest knowledge of the kingdom of God through consistent and reliable miracles of healing. The evidence suggests that we have not "repented and believed the gospel" as Jesus has instructed us to do. Let us now examine Jesus's ministry and his basic teachings (gospel) in greater detail.

2

Jesus's Ministry: An Overview

What did Jesus mean when he proclaims, "The time is fulfilled, and the kingdom of God is at hand: repent ye, and believe the gospel"? (Mark 1:15). This declaration contains the basic theme of Jesus's overall message to the world. To better understand it, we must examine Jesus's opening statement carefully. For us to know anything about God and his kingdom, we must focus intently on Jesus's didactic teachings and on how this knowledge was manifested in Jesus's day-to-day activities in the physical world.

Jesus's birth was predicted by the prophet Isaiah about eight hundred years before his coming (Isaiah 40). In the above declaration, Jesus is confirming that he is the fulfillment of Isaiah's prophecy. He also makes a very perplexing statement when he proclaimed that the kingdom of God was at hand. The majority of people in Jesus's day were certain that the kingdom of God was in heaven—a distant place, far beyond this physical world. Given these beliefs, how are we to decipher what Jesus meant by "the kingdom of God is at hand?"

A kingdom is a political or geographical area ruled by a king or queen. All of the constituents in a kingdom are under the authority of the ruler and bound by the ruler's law. From a spiritual perspective, a kingdom has also been defined as the eternal, spiritual sovereignty of God. Therefore, we can say that the kingdom of God, as Jesus used the concept, can be defined as the place where God is to be found. It is also the place where all the knowledge concerning the kingdom is available, including the rules by which the kingdom and its inhabitants are governed.

According to our current understanding of the kingdom, God, who is sovereign, has full authority over the realm. However, like earthly kings, God also has obligations and responsibilities for the subjects of the kingdom. Jesus seems to be implying that the kingdom of God was inherent in his physical person. As the principal spokesman for the kingdom, Jesus is saying in his initial statement that he is bringing new and important information into the world. He encourages us to repent (or give up our outdated information about God and the kingdom) and accept the truth of the new gospel that he was proclaiming to the world.

Nevertheless, the disciples had great difficulty comprehending the notion that Jesus was the embodiment of God in physical form and that seeing Jesus was the same as seeing God (John 10:30). It would appear that modern-day Christians have an even greater degree of difficulty trying to understand that the full creative power of God was contained within Jesus's physical being. Although this was a very difficult idea for the people of Jesus's time to understand, Jesus was saying, in effect, that "Because I am here with you in the flesh, the kingdom of God is as close to you as I am." Nevertheless, neither the disciples nor the religious authorities could accept the reality that God, with all of his eternal wisdom, majesty, and power, had come to dwell among them for a short period in the person of Jesus.

Jesus's opening statement raises some interesting questions. Do you want to know who or what God is? Do you want to know something about God's true nature? Do you need to know anything about who you are and how God regards you? What do you need to know about true worship or reverence? The answers to all these questions are found in the kingdom of God. In addition to knowing who you are, do you want to know something about your purpose in being here? Then "repent ye, and believe the gospel."

What does Jesus mean by "repent ye?" The first definition of a word in a dictionary is generally the most common meaning or how that particular word is most frequently used in the culture. To repent, in terms of how this word is defined in Christian culture, means to feel remorse, contrition, or self-reproach; or to feel such regret for past conduct as to change one's mind regarding the behavior (Webster's New Collegiate Dictionary). In a religious sense, to repent is to make a change for the better because of remorse, guilt, or contrition for one's sin. However, if we examine the linguistic roots of the word, we come to a slightly different understanding.

The concept of repentance, according to Harper's Biblical Dictionary, is related to the Hebrew word *shub* "which expresses the idea of turning back, retracing one's step in order to return to the right way. In the New Testament, the idea of repentance as turning to the Lord (Heb. *Shurb*) is expressed in the Greek verb *metanoein*. The idea is slightly modified, however, inasmuch as the Greek verb includes the concept of changing one's mind and coming to a new way of thinking (Harper pp 861, pgs 1, 3)."

It appears that this is the sense in which Jesus is saying to repent. It would seem that he is saying "I bring you new knowledge and information about God.

Believe what I am saying and change your way of thinking, or your beliefs about who or what God is. Give up your mistaken ideas about God's true nature, and about who you are and your relationship to him and his kingdom. Change your beliefs and convictions so that you can modify your behavior in your interactions with each other and with the world. Believe the good news that I am declaring to you." This is a reasonable interpretation of Jesus's words because he said, "Repent ye, and believe the gospel" or the good news.

Then, Jesus presented a general overview of the divine curriculum he was ordained to teach the world in his first major teaching seminar; *the Sermon on the Mount.* Included in this initial series of instructions was basic information about God and his responsibilities to all of his children. He used examples from nature—the birds of the air and the lilies of the fields—to make the point that God takes his responsibilities for the well-being of all his children seriously.

Jesus gave us the following assurances: "Therefore I say unto you, take no thought for your life, what you shall eat or what ye shall drink; nor for your body, what you shall put on. Is not the life more than meat, and the body more than raiment? Therefore take no thought saying, 'What shall we eat?' or, 'What shall we drink?' or, 'Wherewithal shall we be clothed?' For your heavenly Father knoweth that ye have need of all these things. But seek ye first the kingdom of God, and his righteousness; and all these things shall be added unto you. Take therefore no thought for the morrow: for the morrow shall take thought for the things of itself. Sufficient unto the day is the evil thereof" (Matt.6:25, 31–34).

Then, in a consistent and spectacular fashion, he healed people afflicted with different diseases and performed other miracles. For example, at the end of two of his great teaching and healing sessions, he created sufficient amounts of food to feed great multitudes of people. On another occasion, he resurrected the only son of a widow out of compassion for her by simply touching the bier (Luke 7:12–15). I believe Jesus began to perform a wide variety of miracles to demonstrate the truth of his words: we should not worry about anything because God, our heavenly Father, was aware of our needs and prepared to meet them. Moreover, through the miracles and healing, Jesus was making the bold statement that he was truly Immanuel: "God who is with us."

Jesus assured us that we need not worry about anything or fear any situation. He tried to impress upon us that God, our perfect Father, was obligated to meet our needs. In the role of God incarnate, Jesus performed routine miracles of healing and exercised control over the physical world as validation of everything he was trying to teach. More importantly, he indicated that God gave him the authority to transfer this knowledge and power to us through his teachings. Jesus said quite clearly, "He who believeth on me, the works that I do he shall do also; and greater works than these shall he do; because I go unto the Father" (John 14:12). To "believe on him" means that every Christian must accept what Jesus is trying to teach us through his words and deeds. And if we believe we "shall" do the greater works of miracles and healing.

The term "shall" is a command that expresses a directive—a word that suggests inevitability. Jesus is clearly saying that healing is one of the things every one of his followers, or those who profess to believe on him, should be doing. Miracles of healing are the "greater works." Nevertheless, it would appear what Jesus was communicating to the world through his teaching and healing ministry has been misinterpreted entirely or misunderstood by the disciples. Furthermore, because of our tendencies to rely on the disciples' reports rather than on Jesus's teachings and instructions, modern-day Christians have also misunderstood the message.

Jesus's basic message to the world is that God, our perfect Father, loves all of his children unconditionally, and that he is committed to providing for all of their needs without restrictions or conditions. Jesus states repeatedly that we simply have to "ask and believe" to have our needs met (Matt.21–22). As a result of the disciples' failure to understand Jesus's basic message, we have lost sight of the importance of healing in our Christian ministries. Furthermore, because we do not routinely practice the healing techniques and practices that Jesus demonstrated for us, we have lost confidence in our abilities to do miracles of healing. There are also some other common beliefs we hold about God, Jesus, sickness, and healing which generate doubt and unbelief which affects our abilities to heal.

Generally, healing in a contemporary church is closely linked to the prevailing religious dogma associated with that particular domination. In most Pentecostal denominations for examples successful healing is subtlety linked with being saved. The implications are that somehow sickness and sin is connected. It was a common belief during Jesus's time that diseases were related to sin and were a punishment from God. Conditions present at birth were believed to be because of the parents' sin or the child's sin in a former life.

These beliefs are clearly illuminated in the scriptures: "And as Jesus passed by, he saw a man which was blind from his birth. And his disciples asked him, saying, 'Master who did sin, this man, or his parents, that he was born blind?' Jesus answered, 'Neither hath this man sinned, nor his parents: but that the works of God should be made manifest in him" (John 9:1–3). Jesus was saying that sometimes we are afflicted with sicknesses or diseases so that healing or "the works of God" should be made manifest in our lives. Jesus appears to be implying that sickness and diseases are simply opportunities for us to manifest God through healing.

When anything is made manifest, it becomes clearly apparent to our sight and our understanding. All of the aspects of the entity are revealed beyond a shadow of a doubt. It is clear and apparent that Jesus is saying to the individual Christian and to the church that one of the purposes of disease is to give us the opportunity to manifest the works of God in the church and in our lives. Actually, Jesus said that the works of God should be manifested through miracles of healing. More-over, the gift of healing should be given to the sick and infirm in our congrega-tions in the same spirit of unconditional love that Jesus manifested in his ministry. Healing and miracles are evidences of God's faithfulness and love for all of his children.

The scripture continues to instruct us on the level of importance Jesus placed on healing. For example, after the disciples informed him that John the Baptist had been beheaded by King Herod, Jesus went to a quiet place in the desert to meditate. However, a great crowd of people followed him there and the report states, "and when Jesus went forth, and saw a great multitude, and was moved with compassion toward them, and he healed their sick" (Matt. 14:14). Healing the sick was always one of Jesus's major priorities. A casual observation of our Christian ministries will reveal, however, that healing does not appear to be as important an aspect of the Church's mission as it was in Jesus's ministry.

Let us consider the manner in which many pastors approach healing in their Sunday morning services. The religious doctrine of many churches defines the issues of sin, salvation, and repentance as the central theme of the gospel of Jesus Christ. Therefore, most sermons focus on doctrines of sin and judgment, issues related to heaven (salvation), and hell (judgment and the punishment for sin). After the sermon has been preached, the first order of business is usually an altar call.

The first call is generally a call to repentance. After that, there will be a call for the sick to come for prayer, if a call for healing is made at all. The message given to the congregation by the order of the altar call is that God wants you to repent of your sins as a first priority. Repentance, according to our theologies and doc-trines, is the first issue, no matter what else may be going on in your life. If, for example, you are dying of cancer, or your child is sick unto death, repenting of your sins is our first priority. The scriptures clearly indicate that this is not the order of priority established by Jesus. Furthermore, there is no evidence in the Bible that Jesus placed any religious or theological conditions on healing other than asking and believing.

The message communicated by the order of the altar call is that the healing of the sick is secondary to our beliefs that they need to repent of their sins or to be "saved." By the time the call for healing is made, doubt has been created in the minds of the afflicted. Furthermore, the altar is now filled with "sinners who need to be saved." Thus, the devoted Christian who happens to be sick is now sharing the altar with those who are sinners and in need of repentance. The sick are made to feel they are sinners who'd better repent, and those who consider themselves saved and sanctified or in fellowship with God feel uncomfortable sharing the alter with those who have been identified as sinners or backsliders. Thus, doubts of worthiness are created by this exclusive initial emphasis on sin and repentance. The scriptures are quite clear that doubt or confusion will severely limit the power of the Holy Spirit to do a work of healing.

This initial focus on sin and repentance imply that you are sick because you have sinned and if you repent, everything you need from God will be granted. The message to the sick person is that they need to comply with our rituals of salvation, accept our doctrines, and then they may be healed. As a result, there is reluctance among the sick to come to the altar for any reason. Even if they come, sufficient doubt has been created in the minds of both the saved and the unsaved at the alter that miracles of healing are very unlikely.

Thus, the not-so-subtle message has been communicated that God is more concerned about issues of salvation, as these issues have been defined in a particular theology or doctrine, than he is about the health and well-being of his children. Because our faith is extremely fragile, doubts and confusion undermine whatever degree of faith or hope may have been generated by the sermon. *A careful analysis of Jesus's teachings will show that there was never a suggestion that there were any conditions attached to healing other than belief.* He demonstrated the importance of healing in his ministry by immediately meeting every healing need or request placed before him!

The records indicate that many of the people of the region had absolute faith that Jesus was willing and able to heal them of any sickness. The lepers, who by law could not mingle with the crowds when Jesus was coming, would cry out with a loud voice, "Jesus, Master, have mercy on us" (Luke 17:13) and Jesus would heal them. The same was true of the blind men. The woman with "the issue of blood" was considered unclean under Jewish law. She was not even supposed to be in the crowd waiting for Jesus. It is recorded that even though she saw many doctors, none of whom were able to heal her condition, she believed that "If I may touch but his clothes, I shall be whole" (Mark 5:28). And she was healed by Jesus. All of these witnesses were certain that Jesus could and would heal them because of what they had seen or because someone with sufficient credibility had told them about Jesus and his ministry of healing, and they believed the reports.

Consequently, in every town and village where Jesus was expected, they gathered all of the sick and infirm in one place where Jesus could heal them. As a first order of business, Jesus would heal them all. I believe the call for healing, as a first priority, is captured beautifully when Jesus said, "Come unto me, all ye that labor and are heavy laden, and I will give you rest. Take my yoke upon you, and learn of me; for I am meek and lowly in heart: and ye shall find rest unto your souls. For my yoke is easy, and my burden is light" (Matt. 11:28–30).

Jesus is saying to us that we can bring all our issues, worries, concerns, and diseases to him, and he will take care of them. He is saying to join with him and learn of him. I believe that he is imploring us to master the information he has given us through his words and actions in the world. I believe that what Jesus means by "my burden is light" is that there is nothing required of you other than that you learn what he is teaching, ask for what you want or need, and believe that you will receive it! He is telling us to repent and change our ways of thinking about God and him.

However, it is impossible to believe that you can get what you need from God if you believe that he is angry with you or if you feel you are bad (sinful) and unworthy. It is quite clear that Jesus gives us a totally different picture of himself and God (meek, lowly in heart, loving, compassionate, etc.) compared to the wrathful God of the Old Testament (remote, judgmental, intolerant, quick to anger, and very dangerous).

In the accounts of many of his most notable healing, the women with the issue of blood, the man born blind, the ten Samaritan lepers for example, there were no indications that Jesus was concerned about anything related to the person other than their need for healing. He simply healed everyone who asked for it or needed it. He healed Jews, Gentiles, heretics (Samaritans), "sinners" (the man who was born blind), heathens (the Canaanite woman's daughter), and the outcasts of society (lepers, madmen, and fallen and disreputable women). Jesus repeatedly demonstrated that a fundamental aspect of God's character is unconditional love and an unwavering commitment to fulfilling his parental responsibility of providing for the needs of all of his children.

What all of the recipients of Jesus's miracles of healing had in common were two levels of faith. Jesus taught them that they were the children of a father whose love for them was unconditional, and they believed him. Secondly, Jesus taught them that they could have anything they needed from God simply by asking and believing. It is apparent that all of the people who flocked to Jesus to be healed believed this also. Their faith, which Jesus inspired through his teaching, healed them and made them whole. *It should be obvious to every Christian, especially leaders and teachers, that we have an obligation to encourage this level of faith in God, and confidence in his unconditional love and commitment to healing any of his children who need it.*

My belief is that we have lost the knowledge and ability to heal the sick with the same degree of certainty as Jesus and some of his followers were able to do. I am speaking of the unnamed healer mentioned in the Gospels of Mark and Luke and the seventy spoken of by Luke. We have lost the ability to inspire sufficient levels of faith in God that the vast multitudes of people afflicted with sicknesses and diseases that medicine cannot heal could come to our churches and be healed. We have failed in our responsibilities to heal at this level because either we do not believe that we have the ability to heal, or we do not feel it is one of our primary responsibilities. We are also very confused about God's true nature and about our relationship with God (perfect Father/beloved son or daughter). Finally, the gospel as it is currently preached throughout the Christian world is so full of contradictions and misinformation about God and his true feeling about us that sufficient levels of doubt and unbelief are generated that consistent healing in our churches become difficult or impossible.

3

Choose Ye This Day

There is much confusion in the world and in Christianity in particular about the true nature of God. Is he the God of the Old Testament, noted for his intolerance for sin and disobedience, and who in his wrath will destroy entire cities, including all the men, women, children, and pets? Or is he the kind and unconditionally loving God, who is infinitely patient, tolerant, and forgiving as Jesus represents him. Is God the perfect Father as Jesus defined him, who is prepared to meet all of the needs of all of his children because of his unconditional and unchanging love for us? (Matt. 6:25–34).

Based on Jesus's instructions, all we need to do to get what we need from our Father is simply to ask and believe we will receive it. Other teachers in the Bible have given us a different version of God. In order for us to be able to inspire sufficient faith to heal consistently, we must decide whether we will follow Jesus's teachings about God and his true nature or continue our current paths of confusion. We also must resolve the dilemma related to Jesus's purpose and function in the world of Christianity.

A fundamental Christian belief is that God's primary purpose in sending Jesus, his only begotten son, was to serve as a sacrifice for our sins. Therefore our focus on Jesus as the "Sacrificial Lamb" diminishes the importance of his teachings and his miracles of healing in our theologies and doctrines. This was the disciples' interpretation of the crucifixion and the central thesis of what Luke defined as the "Apostles' Doctrine" (Acts 2:42). The belief that God required a blood sacrifice as atonement for sin was based on the ancient beliefs of the people of the Old Testament. However, these beliefs were not unique to the people of that region. The idea of "blood sacrifice" has long been an active force in human history. Yet long before Jesus's time, the prophet Micah had already addressed this issue of sacrifice in a very direct way when he said:

"Wherewith shall I come before the Lord, and bow myself before the high God? Shall I come before him with burnt offerings, with calves of a year old? Will the Lord be pleased with thousands of rams, or with ten thousands of rivers of oil? Shall I give my firstborn for my transgression, the fruit of my body for the sin of my soul? He hath shewed thee O man, what is good; and what doth the Lord require of thee, but to do justly, and to love mercy, and to walk humbly with thy God?" (Micah 6:6–8).

The prophet Micah was preparing the people of God for a dramatic change in their thinking about God and his relationship with humanity. Many of the old gods required a blood sacrifice as a means of earning favor or for the appeasement of transgressions. Archaeological evidence of sacrificing the firstborn child to placate the gods has been uncovered in the region when the tiny skeletons of newborn babies were discovered embedded in the foundations of homes. Old ideas and beliefs are difficult to give up or change.

We are all familiar with the story of Abraham and Isaac (Gen. 22:1–18) that is closely related to these ancient beliefs and practices. The irony of this story is that its basic premise centers on the belief that a loving God would require a devoted father, Abraham, to sacrifice his only son as a means of gaining favor or as an expiation of sin. It would seem even more unlikely that that it was a test of obedience, being that God already knew who Abraham was and how he was likely to behave in this particular circumstance. Abraham already had a strong track record of obedience to God. Nevertheless, the fact that Abraham appeared to be willing to kill his son in a bloody, ritualistic murder at the behest of God is a powerful example of the kind of beliefs Jesus wanted the people of his day to abandon in favor of what he was telling us about God's true nature.

Micah seems to suggest that it is really a strange belief that God would be swayed by any kind of material or ritualistic sacrifice from us. He asserts that our attitudes and behaviors toward each other are what God is concerned about. In the Sermon on the Mount, Jesus reinforces Micah's point when he connects us to the basic themes Micah presented. He begins this important block of instructions on the basic principles and practice of Christianity with "Blessed are the poor in spirit for theirs is the kingdom of heaven" (Matt. 5:1). He also tells us "Blessed are the meek: for they shall inherit the earth" and "Blessed are the merciful: for they shall obtain mercy" (Matt. 5:5, 7).

Jesus is saying that the sacrifices God requires are not material. God, our perfect Father, requires humility in our spirit (attitudes) and meekness in our behavior. God, who is the great "I Am," is whole and complete in his being and could not possibly "need" anything material from us! Jesus simply said to repent or give up the old ideas and beliefs about God, and "learn of me." In doing so, you will learn of God. He seems to say, "Receive the knowledge and information I am giving you about who I am and about what it is possible for you to become. Learn of me, and you will learn all that you need to know about God."

Through his teaching and example, Jesus gives us a different concept of God than what was commonly believed at that time. For example, sickness and poverty were prevalent conditions in the world during Jesus's time. Therefore, miracles of healing were very real and powerful expressions of God's presence in the life of the individual, and as such, they were defined by Jesus as evidence that "the kingdom of God is come nigh unto you" (Luke 10:9).

The fundamental message conveyed by a miracle was that God is not in some far, unreachable place, but is as close to you as the healing touch from one who had been sent by him. The second important point was that God, your heavenly Father, loves you unconditionally and does not require intermediaries, elaborate rituals, ceremonies, and sacrifices to be reached. The third point was that as a perfect Father, God has real obligations to you, as does any responsible parent (Matt. 7:9–11). Parental responsibilities and obligations to their children are not in any way subject to how the children behave. Human parents have the responsibility to provide for their children's need. These parental obligations extend to all of our children equally—both the "good" and obedient children and the "bad" and disobedient children.

Miracles of healing are a means of bridging the perceptual gap between the Father and his children. If you ask someone where God is, the response is usually "in heaven." If your next question is where is heaven, the first inclination would be to point up toward the sky. You would get this response because most people in the Christian world believe that God is in heaven. Heaven is thought to be a distant place, far beyond our physical universe and beyond our abilities to reach directly. This belief about the location of the kingdom of God persists despite Jesus's insistence that God, who is believed to be in heaven, is within (Luke 17:21). Even though Jesus said it, we do not believe it. We don't believe Jesus because our minds cannot comprehend how the kingdom of God could literally be within us. We cannot conceive of the truth of what Jesus said to us because it is difficult for us to believe that we are spiritual rather than physical beings.

Jesus also referred to God as a perfect Father who loves all of his children equally and unconditionally (Matt. 5:43–48). The disciples could not understand this notion or conceptualization of God and neither does the average Christian. I believe that any characterization of God which is contradictory to Jesus's teachings about God's nature is essentially wrong. Nevertheless, any objective analysis of Christian theology will show that we have misinterpreted what Jesus said about God. We have given equal weight to what Jesus says about our perfect Father and his true nature and what the disciples, patriarchs, prophets, and scribes of the Old Testament reported about God, his character and nature.

The God of the Old Testament was a fearful father who required strict obedience to all of the "rules" under the threat of death and destruction. He was also a God who had a "chosen" or special group of people whom he favored above his other children. But Jesus said, "I and my Father are one" (John 10:30). There was nothing in Jesus's character to suggest that he was anything other than unconditionally loving to all of God's children, including Jews, Samaritans, and Gentiles. Therefore, God's character and nature had to be the same as Jesus's character and nature. Consistent with the apostles' error, the perfect loving father Jesus represented became a God of fear and retribution in the disciples' minds and doctrine (Acts 3:13–23); and this fundamental theological error has been passed down through the generations to the present time.

In the Revelation of John, Jesus, who was unconditionally loving, kind and, gentle, and who demonstrated infinite patience and tolerance, mutates into a fierce warrior-king riding on a white horse and armed with a double-edged sword. Jesus, the Prince of Peace, is transformed into the ultimate warrior-king who will lead the army of God against the forces of evil (Rev. 19:1–21). This may make sense according to our theology, but the reality of an unchanging God contradicts this notion.

It is remarkable that we would believe that a God who could speak a world into existence would need to resort to a destructive war to eliminate evil from the world. If eradicating evil from the world, as we understand the term, was this important to God, I know a less complicated way of accomplishing this goal. God could simply speak it out of existence, and it would be done! God could also give us an infallible power to discern it, and we could speak it out of existence.

There is a logical justification for John's interpretation of his vision. He was over ninety years old at that time and living in a deprived and isolated state. By the time his revelations were written, he probably had forgotten much of what he knew about God through his experiences with Jesus. But because we have a much broader perspective of Jesus's Gospel than John's, we have to be cognizant of these glaring contradictions and their role in creating fear, doubt, and unbelief.

There is ample information in the Sermon on the Mount to conclude that Jesus is trying to teach us that there are no real justifications for conflict, violence, and killing on our part (Matt. 5:21–26). There is nothing in the story of Jesus's life and teaching to suggest that there were any contradictions between what he taught about conflict and violence and the manner in which he handled conflict in his life and through his ministry (see Luke 9:51–56; Matt. 26:47–53).

When Jesus said, "And if any man will sue thee at the law, and take away thy coat, let him have thy cloak also" (Matt. 5:40), Jesus makes it clear that even when you know that you are right about something, you should not get into conflict or fight about it. Jesus is reminding us that a child of God has no enemies worthy of hate, fear, or conflict, and there are no issues among us that we should be fighting about. If this be the case, then how could God, the sovereign of the universe, have adversaries worthy of destructive warfare? Nevertheless, the disciples and many modern Christians do not understand what Jesus was trying to teach us. Thus it seems we are more comfortable serving the Old Testament God than the perfect Father of all humanity of whom Jesus spoke.

Theologically speaking, modern-day Christians have not yet fully resolved these fundamental contradictions about God's true nature. In the exultations of our sermons, we switch from one version of God to the other when it is convenient for our doctrinal purposes. We are willing to negate the basic truth of an unchanging God in service to our particular doctrine or theology. Thus, we create confusion about God's true nature, which generates doubt, fear, and unbelief in the minds and hearts of his children. We must remember that doubt had the power to stifle Jesus's ability to do miracles (great work) in the area in which he grew up, where everyone knew him as Joseph's son. They doubted that he could be the Son of God or a divine being and it is written, "He did not many mighty works there because of their unbelief" (Matt. 13:58).

The time has come for Christians to, in the words of Joshua, "Choose ye this day whom you will serve" (Josh. 24:15). Will it be the God of the patriarchs, apostles, prophets, scribes, publicans, and Pharisees? Is the God we serve the multifaceted, sectarian God of our ideologies, theologies, and doctrines? Or will it be God as Jesus has defined him by his gentle, kind, and loving behavior in the world, and through his teaching and miracles of healing? We can no longer maintain the notion of a dual God—a God of unconditional love and a God of fear and judgment. There are no scriptural justifications for maintaining this position because Jesus said, "I and my Father are one" (John 10:30).

4

Greater Works

The majority of us have two related and persistent fears. We are afraid that we will contract an ailment that doctors will be unable to cure, and, then we will die painful and lingering deaths. I am certain that in Jesus's time, this was also a common fear. According to the reports, Jesus went about healing all kinds of sicknesses and diseases throughout Israel, Judea, and Samaria. He had control over the physical world: he walked on water when he needed to get to the other side of the lake, raised Lazarus from the dead, and calmed a raging storm with a simple command.

Jesus performed miracles to demonstrate that God's divine power and protection were available to us in any situation of fear or danger. He was also trying to teach that the Spirit of God was inherent in our being, as we are children created in God's own image. Children have the genetic makeup of their parents. There is nothing they will ever do that will make them be genetically different from their parents. Therefore, spiritually, we have God-potential in us by our very nature. Even though Jesus said that we are the children of a perfect Father, we find this difficult to believe. We do not understand what it truly means to be a child of God.

We can behave as if the inherent power of God is not a part of our being. We can deny that the Holy Spirit dwells within us because of what we have been taught about who we are, and our inherent unworthiness in the sight of God. But nothing can alter the fact that we are created in God's own image and likeness. Jesus confirmed the presence of God and the power inherent in us when he said, "At that day ye shall know that I am in my Father, and ye in me, and I in you" (John 14:20). Jesus, the Word of God made flesh, is in all of us. How do we know this? If we believe the scripture, then we know this to be true because Jesus said it without any qualifications. Jesus is the Word made flesh, and if we integrate Jesus's words into our being (believe on him), then Jesus abides in us with the full creative power of God in the form of his words and the Holy Spirit.

Jesus was trying to teach us that faith is the key to gaining access to the power to heal diseases and perform miracles. I also believe that spiritual power can only be used consistently to do those things that reflect God in the physical world because God must be manifested in Spirit and in truth. Jesus always healed those who needed or requested it. Acts of healing were an expression of God's unconditional love for those who needed healing and requested it. There is ample scriptural evidence that Jesus expected us to carry on his healing tradition.

An important element in Jesus's teaching ministry was his instruction to us about our obligations to heal the sick. Jesus said that "He that believeth on me, the works that I do shall he do also; and greater works than these shall he do" (John 14:12). I believe that he meant this quite literally. This statement implies that we have the responsibility for healing the sick; but it also means that we have the inherent ability to heal. *Thus, any Christian who professes to "believe on the Lord Jesus," should be able to do the things that he did.* However, I do not know of any church where we can send a relative with a diagnosis of cancer, for example, and have a reasonable expectation that they will be healed. Nor do we know of anyone who can consistently do the "greater works" or routinely heal all manners of sicknesses and diseases.

I am not saying there is no healing in the church, nor am I saying there are no Christians with the gift of healing. We have all seen the healing power of God manifested in churches, and many church members have testified about the miracles in their lives. But generally, there are no Christians doing the "greater works" (miracles of healing) consistently enough that the average church is known as a place where ordinary people can come to be healed. This is especially true if the sick fall into the category of those who have been classified by our theology and doctrine as sinners.

Even when specific prayers for healing are available, they are generally offered within a doctrinal context with strings attached. Because the majority of sermons focus on a particular version of sin and repentance, it would appear to the sick and infirmed in the congregation that God is a sectarian and conditional God. Thus, healing appears to be contingent upon repentance as defined by the doctrine! We know this is false because there are many true believers in our congregations who are suffering and dying from sicknesses and diseases. The result, in the minds of the sick, is doubts and unbelief that blocks the flow of healing. This much is certain: the conditional God taught by Christian theology is quite unlike God as Jesus defined him.

Let me digress for a moment and share a personal experience to illustrate this point. During the latter stages of my active addiction, my pattern was binge drinking. As I mentioned, I contemplated suicide many times, and I knew, since the pain was so intense, that eventually I would be compelled to act on this impulse. However, what kept me from killing myself was the knowledge that my family loved me. I had some concerns about the trauma my suicidal death would cause them, so I held on.

I went to church many times looking for the possibilities of hope and healing. I also went to the altar frequently to receive prayers for healing! There were good people there, including my mother, who prayed for me. The sanctuary at the altar is often defined as the "throne of grace." But I was unable to find what I needed there. The prayers of the people of the congregation were that I would be converted or saved rather than be healed. Their belief, based on what I know about Pentecostalism, was that my suffering was related to my status of "sinner." Therefore to be healed, it was being subtly suggested that I needed to be "saved" first. But I knew, however, that the rituals of salvation could not heal the sickness of the soul that afflicted me from childhood. And there is nothing in the records of Jesus's healing ministry that would indicate that God required repentance as a condition for healing.

One fateful day I came to the place within myself where I knew that healing had to come, or I would surely die. So I did what my parents trained me to do in times of trouble: I prayed a simple prayer. I said, "God, I cannot live this way, I must have help!" God answered my prayer without conditions when he told me to call Alcoholics Anonymous. When I made the call, a stranger took me to an AA meeting that night. As drunk as I was, in this place among strangers who were the equivalent of biblical publicans and sinners, I found what I had been unable to find in church. I found salvation in the form of hope, and I found God!

The God I found was the same God spoken of by Jesus: God, the perfect Father who loves *all* of his children unconditionally. I was given a gift of healing over time that was beyond anything that I could have ever imagined. I know that my healing was a greater work or a miracle, because if the healing that occurred in my mind, body, and spirit had happened in the "twinkling of an eye," or in a single moment, it would qualify as a miracle of the same order as Jesus's healing of the man who was born blind or any of his other miracles of healing. And in the process of healing over time, I did repent in that I changed my thinking about God and Jesus, and about myself.

Be that as it may, Jesus drew huge crowds of people everywhere he went. A major factor in his notoriety was that his reputation as a reliable healer and miracle-worker preceded him wherever he went. I am certain that anyone who saw or heard of Jesus would say to anyone who was sick, "If you can just get to Jesus, he will heal you." If the response was, "I don't know, the doctor said I am going to die," or "nobody can heal blindness, madness, or leprosy," the faithful person would reply, "I don't care what the doctors said. I know that if you get to Jesus, he will heal you."

If there were any doubts about Jesus's willingness or ability to heal because of issues like race, creed, social class, or moral character, the response would be that it does not matter to Jesus if you are a Roman, a heathen, a sinner, a Samaritan, or any of the many categories that we have been taught separates us from God's love and healing power. They would be informed that Jesus said they are worthy children of God and be encouraged to come to Jesus and be healed.

Perhaps the one who knew the truth about Jesus would begin to tell stories about him and his miracles of healing. These stories would be told with such fervor and conviction that those who were sick and diseased would come to believe that if they can just get to Jesus, they will be healed. Many of the people healed by Jesus were not very religious. The religious authorities of that day defined them as "publicans and sinners." Among those who were healed and ministered to were women, children, lepers, madmen, and Samaritans, who, by the way, the Jews believed were unclean heretics destined for hell.

I know if there were individual Christians who could consistently do the "greater works" of healing or churches with reliable healing ministries where anyone would feel comfortable attending, the sick and diseased would come to be healed, just as they did in Jesus's day. People with cancer, AIDS, asthma, diabetes—any of the conditions that medicine has trouble healing, including sicknesses of the mind and spirit (demonic possessions)—would eventually come in such numbers that walls could not contain them. They would come as the lepers came with the stench of their sores. They would come as the unwashed madmen came. They all came to Jesus for healing just as they were, and he gladly received them and healed them. Moreover, the record states that Jesus healed them without conditions other than faith or belief

It should be obvious from our history that the Christian church is not doing the greater works of miracles of healing. In fact, when a powerful healer appears in a congregation, the healing activity is generally shunted into a quiet place within the congregation where hopefully, it will not be too noticeable. *It is as if mainline Christianity has totally rejected healing as an essential aspect of the church's overall mission to the world.* Thus, we have rejected an important element of the gospel of Jesus Christ.

5

Why the Greater Works Are Not Being Done

We are not doing the "greater works" as Jesus promised we should be doing them through the church because Christians are confused about too many things. We are confused about God's true nature. For example, is he God as Jesus represents him, or is he the God of the Old Testament as Peter defined him in his early sermons? Do we believe a contradictory combination of Old and New Testament theology in which all good things are attributed to God but the devil is blamed when we do, in fact, ask and not receive? How do we explain why a true believer's basic needs are not being met, such as poor children in third world countries starving to death or dedicated church members in the prime of life dying rather than being routinely healed in our churches?

We are also confused about who or what Jesus is. Is Jesus the Word made flesh who came from heaven to reveal the truth about God, or did he come to create more rules to control our lives for some other purpose? A more basic question is related to Jesus's divinity. Is Jesus God incarnate, or is he "Jesus of Nazareth, a man approved of God," as Peter defines him in his second major sermon? (Acts 2:22).

There is confusion about who we are and how God regards us. Are we, for example, God's imperfect children who, according to the Old Testament prophet, "are all as an unclean thing, and all our righteousness are as filthy rags"? (Isaiah 64:6). Or do we define ourselves as Jesus did: beloved children of a perfect Father. He assures us we should not be worried about anything because God can be trusted to take care of all of our basic needs regardless of how we think or behave in the world (Matt. 6:25–34).

Whose report should we believe? Should a Christian believe and teach what Jesus taught us about God and his relationship with his children when he said, "If ye then, being evil, know how to give good gifts unto your children, how much more shall your Father which is in heaven give good things to them that ask him?" (Matt. 7:11). Are there more authoritative teachers in the Bible than Jesus? Do the patriarchs, prophets, scribes, apostles, and theologians, *none* of whom had ever seen God, know more about God than Jesus did?

We cannot develop a sufficient level of trust in God until we have resolved our confusion about these basic issues. Moreover, not seeing Jesus as our only teacher and guide concerning God and the kingdom of heaven has hindered our ability to fully understand the essence of his teaching. We have also lost sight of the importance of healing in the ministry of Jesus Christ, and as a result, we have lost the knowledge of how miracles of healing are achieved.

Jesus had total access to the full powers of creation. God gave him this power because he could be trusted not to abuse it in any way. Through the power of his will he could make anything *be* whatever he wanted it to be. He had total control over the physical world, as he demonstrated in the miracles of the fish and loaves and the calming of the sea.

Jesus had a perfect sense of order and knowledge of the true nature of being. This knowledge gave him an understanding of the nature of infirmities. Jesus demonstrated his power in his ministry by healing every known human condition. Moreover, he reminded us who we are and what our potentials are when he plainly said, "Verily, verily, I say unto you, He that believeth on me, the works that I do shall he do also; and greater works than these shall he do; because I go unto my Father" (John 14:12).

The question we must answer is why there are none among us who have conclusively demonstrated a consistent ability to do the greater works about which Jesus spoke? We do not have access to the power to continually do the "greater works" of healing cancer or any other affliction modern medicine cannot heal because we lack faith in God, faith in ourselves and in the inherent worthiness of our brothers and sisters. We cannot access this power because we are judgmental, intolerant, impatient, and unforgiving. We do not know how to love one another unconditionally. We are confused about whether Jesus was simply a special man approved by God or whether he was as he defined himself: God incarnate.

Another problem is that we cannot be trusted to use the power of God to serve only his will and purposes because we lack wisdom. Any objective analysis of the Acts of the Apostles and the history of the early universal (Catholic) church will provide a sad commentary of how the early Christian leaders, following a theology based on the Old Testament's version of the God of Abraham, Isaac and Jacob, used the power of God through the Holy Spirit to coerce, intimidate, torture, and kill those who violated the rules the disciples and early church fathers created and attributed to God. These historic evil deeds of the early church conclusively prove how completely the disciples and early Christian leaders misunderstood, misinterpreted, and misrepresented the gospel of Jesus Christ. Hypocrisy, murder, torture, slavery, racial discrimination, genocide, and the perpetuation of religious dogma as scientific fact (i.e., the world is flat) are a part of the historical legacy of the Roman Catholic Church, which is the mother church of every Christian.

Even today who, among the most holy human beings you know, could be trusted with "all power in heaven and earth" that Jesus was given by God? Think of the most noted religious leaders of our day. What do you think any of these individuals would do with the power and authority Jesus had in his time on earth? Do you truly believe that God could trust any current religious leader with the full power of creation and still have any degree of certainty they would not abuse it? Would you trust any of the leaders you see on your television screens with the power Jesus had?

Because of our religious ideologies concerning sin and salvation and our commitments to our theological belief systems, members of most religious groups believe two things: theirs is the true path, and they have a mandate from God to proselytize anyone who does not follow their way ("unbelievers"). The best leaders of any religious group, in accordance with their theological beliefs, would certainly use the power and authority given by God to compel others to believe as they do. It is also quite likely they would use this power to mandate what they believed to be appropriate behavior in the world. History is a witness that religious leaders with secular and spiritual authority will use power to coerce, intimidate, punish, or even kill those who do not believe as they do or behave the way they believe people should behave.

Remember the story of the prophet Elisha, who requested a double portion of Elijah's spirit? After God granted his request, Elisha smote the Jordan with Elijah's mantle and the waters parted. His second miracle was the healing of the bitter waters of the well at Jericho. Shortly thereafter, he used the power God had granted him to call forth two female bears to kill forty-two children who had mocked him (2 Kings 2:1–24). This behavior was acceptable under the belief system associated with the God of Abraham, Isaac, and Jacob. However, it would be inconceivable for a true follower of Christ to kill a child for any reason, because the idea of killing another human being for any reason was alien to Jesus's character and nature.

Jesus had the authority to compel us to believe any religious doctrine he or God considered important. However, there is no biblical evidence that Jesus was ever tempted to use his power to compel us to do anything or that Jesus used the power inherent in his being to hurt anyone. He certainly had the power to protect himself from the false accusations and physical abuse during his trial and crucifixion. His response to his pending torture and crucifixion was to say, "Nevertheless not my will, but thine, be done" (Luke 22:42). Even under extreme provocation as he was mocked while dying on the cross, Jesus remained faithful to God's will and purpose. He was consistent to his teaching of peace, love, and nonviolence and to God's fundamental values and integrity as they were expressed in his life and teaching. He said, "Father forgive them; for they know not what they do" (Luke 23:34).

Jesus had the strength of character, love, and patience needed to teach us by words and example what is required if we are to be fully trusted with the power of creation. He also gave us a comprehensive course of study that we must complete if we are to achieve a sufficient level of spiritual maturity and be given access to the full power of creation and the ability "to think or speak" whatever we want or need into being.

At the end of that great seminar known as the Sermon on the Mount, Jesus reminded us, saying, "Therefore whosoever heareth these sayings of mine, and doeth them, I will liken him unto a wise man, which built his house upon a rock" (Matt. 7:24). Knowledge of God's true nature and purpose for the children created in his image and likeness is the "rock" upon which we must build our Christian character. *Christ is the model for a Christian's life and behavior in the world!*

Jesus is saying that how we behave toward each other in our daily lives is more important than our commitment to ideologies, doctrines, and flawed belief systems. Above all else, he emphasized there is an essential ability we must master before we can have access to God's power. We must thoroughly understand what he is trying to teach us, beginning with his first requirement for a true Christian life when he said, "A new commandment I give unto you, That ye love one another; as I have loved you, that ye also love one another. By this shall all men know that ye are my disciples, if ye have love one to another" (John 13:34–35).

Until we have a more comprehensive understanding of the lessons Jesus was trying to teach us, it will be impossible for the Father to permit us to have access to the power to heal and to perform miracles in a routine manner. To learn what Jesus was trying to teach, we must be willing to challenge our fundamental theology and look at the entire story from a different perspective.

6

The Gift of Healing

As I mentioned, I grew up in the fundamentalist religious culture of Georgia during the late 1930s and early 1940s. My father was a minister in the early days of Pentecostalism and the Churches of God in Christ. I have been active in a Pentecostal church since 1986. In my life, I have had enough firsthand experiences with life-changing events and miracles to know that God is real, and his love is unconditional.

My recovery from alcoholism and the healing of the underlying psychological conditions (depressive neurosis, suicidal ideation, chronic anxiety, and insomnia) that plagued my life from early childhood have given me firsthand knowledge of miracles and God's healing power. Although I have not had any academic training as a psychotherapist, I have had a thirty-year career as a therapist/director of an employee-counseling program in a large and prestigious medical center in New York City. As a pioneer in the substance abuse field and the newly evolved field of employee assistance programs, I have made major contributions including journal articles and book chapters. During my career, I have also been an adjunct professor at three local universities, SUNY at Stony Brook, Long Island University at Dobbs Ferry, and Mercy College. My professional career has been replete with miracles, but that's a story for another time.

My life experience has taught me that twelve-step programs are powerful spiritual paths through which miracles of healing are routine occurrences. We know that God is in the twelve step rooms all over the world because his power is directly made manifest among us. Recovery is what AA members call this spiritual path through which God manifests himself in the lives of alcoholics and drug addicts.

Recovery is an ongoing process of emotional, physical, and spiritual healing that takes place through learning spiritual concepts like faith in God, patience, tolerance, service, and unconditional love of both self and others. It is also a program of sustained emotional and spiritual growth. One of the lessons learned on this path is that God is a perfect and faithful father who is attentive to the needs of all of his children—including a group morally corrupt and sinful beyond measure according to any accepted standard. Nonetheless, God delivers them out of the pain and darkness of addictions without any prior conditions other than seeking, finding, and believing.

God gives grace, mercy, and healing to his children from every race, creed, color, and moral persuasion. This includes atheists, agnostics, homosexuals, thieves, murderers, adulterers, and unrepentant sinners of every stripe. Healing is only possible through the witness of those in recovery and the faith generated through stories of deliverance and healing. The article of faith in twelve-step programs is that the source of healing is "a power greater than ourselves," believed by most to be God as we understand him. I have discovered on this spiritual path that God is merciful and full of surprises and wonders.

In the early 1980s, God began to prepare me for another "surprise and wonder" in my spiritual journey. Some of my clients who were receiving therapy began to reveal to me special healing needs, and the Holy Spirit began to instruct me to pray for their conditions, and by prayer and faith God healed them.

In March 1985, a long-term client came for her appointment. She was a fifty-year-old Irish Catholic nurse and an ex-nun with many family issues, including chronic anger related to judgment and the inability to forgive. When she came to my office on this particular morning, she had a leather cuff on her right wrist. I asked her what was wrong, and she replied that she had carpal tunnel syndrome. She explained the condition and said she was scheduled to have surgery the following week to remove the calcium deposits from the carpal tunnel and relieve the pressure on the nerves that control the hand. When I asked her if the surgery would fix the condition, she replied that the doctors were not certain that the operation would successfully heal her, but they decided to do the surgery because the pain in her wrist and numbness in her hand were becoming more severe.

We began the therapy and about halfway through the session, the Holy Spirit said to me, "Pray for her hand." I thought, "Pray for her hand?" The Spirit repeated, quite calmly, "Pray for her hand." I ended the session about five minutes early and very nervously asked my client, "Would you like me to pray for your hand?" I was surprised when she replied, "I was hoping you would ask me that."

I asked her to stretch out her hand: then holding my hands above and below her hand and wrist, I said a very short, silent prayer of healing. When I finished the prayer, she moved her fingers around and flexed the hand. I asked her what was happening. She said she felt a warm, tingling sensation in her hand. I replied that this was a good sign because something was going on in the hand and wrist.

She called me during the middle of the following week, very excited. She told me she had just returned from a visit with her surgeon, who ordered a second X-ray when she reported that the pain and numbness in her hand had diminished. The film indicated that the calcium buildup in her wrist, that had compressed the carpal tunnel causing pressure and damage to the nerves regulating her hand, had disappeared. The condition was healed.

She said that the doctor asked her what happened. My first response was a panicky: "You did not tell him, did you?" She replied, "Of course I did." She stated the surgeon told her that he had the original X-ray report clearly showing the calcium deposits in her wrist and the compressed carpal tunnel. The second X ray just as clearly revealed that the deposits disappeared. His other comment was, "You received a miracle of healing—enjoy it!"

A few weeks later, a 38-year-old male came to see me for the first time. He was a supervisor in the nutrition department and had had a serious accident in the kitchen of the hospital about three years before. He slipped on a wet spot and ruptured a couple of disks in his spine. As a result, he was totally paralyzed in both legs. Eventually, he had an operation on his spine, and after a period of painful physical therapy and rehabilitation, regained the use of his legs.

As the incision healed, however, scar tissue infiltrated into the spinal cord, causing intense pain in his back and numbness in his legs. The doctors were reluctant to operate on his spine again because of the risk of permanent paralysis. Additionally, there was persistent pain in his lower spine that was so intense that he was sent to a specialist in the pain clinic, and was taking massive dosages of painkillers. A psychiatrist was also treating him for anxiety and depression with suicidal ideation.

On our third visit, he came into my office walking very gingerly. When he sat down, he winced. I asked him what was wrong. He told me that the sciatica nerve in his right leg was inflamed and when he sat down, his pant leg brushing against his skin caused an intense burning pain in the leg. During the session, the Holy Spirit again spoke to me and said, "Pray for his leg!" I ended the session early and asked him, quite nervously, "Do you believe in God?" He said, "Of course I do. If it were not for God and Saint Christopher, I would be dead. I had three serious car accidents and only survived by the grace of God." I asked him if he wanted me to pray for his leg. He said, "I think that is a marvelous idea."

I did not physically touch him but moved both hands down the side of the leg as I said a silent prayer of healing. He could feel the flow of energy (healing virtue) moving through his leg. Then, I was moved by the Holy Spirit to pray for his back (spinal cord). I directed him to stand up and gently laid my hands on his back over the lower spine. I did not say a conscious prayer but simply opened myself to the guidance of the Spirit. After a few seconds, we ended the session, and he left my office.

He called me on the telephone a couple of days later and said that before he leaves for work every morning, he feeds his pets. He was running late, and as he rushed out to his car, he remembered that he left his lab coat in the house. He returned to the house and while reaching for the knob on the front door, suddenly became aware that the pain was gone from his back and his legs.

Before reporting to work, he had several appointments that morning: one with his psychiatrist and another at the pain clinic. The staff of the clinic could tell by the way he walked and by his affect that something significant had happened. When they asked, he told everyone his counselor had prayed for him and his back and legs were healed. The pain was gone. Everyone who saw him that day could tell by the bounce in his step that something important had happened. When they asked what it was, he told them. I was becoming very uncomfortable and nervous about all of this notoriety in my work setting, and I had some serious questions about where all of this might lead.

During our next session, he told me that one of the workers in his unit asked him if I would give her an appointment and pray for a very painful chronic arthritic knee. She was an elderly Jamaican woman who worked in the hospital for many years. He said, "Of course he will," and gave her my telephone number. Her intention was to call me the following morning for an appointment. When she awoke the next morning, the pain was gone from her knee. The condition was healed by her faith that she could or would be healed.

Her healing resulted from a sequence of thoughts that initiated a healing process. What I mean is that there was a sequence of thoughts in her mind that led her to conclude that if it happened for another person, it was possible that it (healing) will happen for her. Seeing the man who was healed generated sufficient faith that there was a man of God who can initiate miracles of healing and her intent to take specific action on the following morning were enough to initiate a healing process: and the condition was healed by faith by morning. I believe that this is the same healing dynamic or process which powered or generated healing faith in Jesus's day.

A few weeks later, I received a telephone call from another patient. She was in the hospital suffering from a kidney condition. She made the call on a Monday morning. I wasn't able to visit her that day because of a busy schedule, but we continued to communicate by telephone. On Wednesday, she was very depressed when she called and informed me that her kidneys were failing. The doctors did not know why her kidney functions were deteriorating, and they were unable to halt the process. The hospital social worker had spoken with her that day about dialysis, and she was informed that they had placed her name on the national registry of patients in need of a kidney transplant. I was finally able to visit her on Friday of that week.

This woman had been in therapy with me for over two years and had an interesting history. She was married to a man in her church whose father was the pastor of one of the local churches. She had been very active in various ministries in the church but began to withdraw from these activities when she and her husband began to have serious marital problems. Her husband, who was a junior pastor in his father's church, was physically abusive and very domineering. The family was also having financial problems because he was unwilling to find steady work. As a result, she began to drift away from the church and act out in various ways. All of her acting-out behavior was defined by church doctrine as sin.

The canon of her church, based on Old Testament laws and traditions, required that women and children submit to the authority of the husband. Although she was a good mother and the primary wage earner in this family, she felt unappreciated and unloved because of the way her husband treated her. It was especially difficult for her to understand why her church family would give their tacit support and approval to her husband when he was physically abusive, failed in his primary responsibilities as breadwinner, and did not treat her and the children in a loving Christian way.

In the initial therapy with her, I tried to teach that she was precious in the sight of God and that his love for her was unconditional. I suggested that she should not confuse church dogma with what God thought about her. I told her that, according to Jesus's teaching, God meets the basic needs of both his "just and unjust" children. I suggested to her that God loved her very much and wanted the best for her despite what she thought or felt about her worthiness based on her "religious state" or her current behavior. But after two years of therapy, there was little if any changes in her behavior.

In her sick room on that fateful Friday, we spoke for a short while. Finally, I said to her, "I guess we need to pray for your kidneys." I asked her to relax and close her eyes. She was sitting up in her bed, so I held my hands over her kidneys and said a very brief prayer of healing. When I said amen, she opened her eyes and said to me, "Mr. Hudson, I know that you did not physically touch me, but I felt the pressure of hands on my kidneys." At that moment, I felt physically drained of energy. I said that I believed something special was happening and that she should have faith in God.

She called me at home on Saturday. She told me that her doctors were puzzled by the results of the latest test that indicated that her blood values were improving. According to their knowledge, her kidneys had been dying and the process was irreversible. Nevertheless, the results of the most recent tests suggested that her dying kidneys had begun to function again. Although they did not quite understand what had happened, her doctors told her that if her kidneys continued to improve, they were going to discharge her from the hospital in a couple of days. I came to work the following Monday and did not hear from her until about six o'clock that evening. She very excitedly told me she was home and that her kidneys were functioning normally.

This young woman, who was considered to be an unrepentant sinner, had been given a miracle of healing by her Father whose love for her was unconditional. I believe that an important factor in her healing was that as the instrument God used to heal her, I believed that she was worthy to have whatever she needed from God, based on what Jesus had said. Because I believed in her and treated her with love and respect, she trusted me and what I taught her about God. I was also able to inspire a healing level of faith (belief) in her based on my interpretation of what I believe Jesus taught us about himself, God, and about ourselves.

About a month later, my niece, who is an evangelist in COGIC, drove to Georgia to visit with her mother. Her mother, who is my youngest sister, drove back to Yonkers with her to visit for a few days. My family and I stopped by to visit them a couple of days later. When we arrived at the house, my niece was lying in bed in a dark room with a wet towel covering her eyes and forehead. She stated that she had been suffering with a very severe case of vertigo or "car sickness" since her arrival.

She remained in bed during our visit but got up to say good-bye when we were ready to leave. I hugged her and just before walking out of the door, the Holy Spirit moved me to gently cup her face in my hands and pray for her condition. After a few seconds, I released her. The vertigo was instantly healed. She looked up with surprise and gently shook her head slowly from side to side. I asked her, "What are you doing…looking for the vertigo? It's gone."

Both she and her mother had this curious expression on their faces that seemed to ask "how did he do that?" They are traditionally saved and sanctified Pentecostals who have questions and doubts about who I am and about my relationship with God. They know that like the unnamed healer, I am one who, in the words of John and James, "followeth not us!" I am not the typical "born–

again" in terms of ideology, theology, and practice. They still have doubts or questions about why God would use me in this manner when there have never been any outward manifestations or signs that I am "saved and sanctified, and filled with the Holy Ghost." I sometimes have questions and doubts myself about why I have been given this gift. Nevertheless, the story continues.

7

Healing in the Secular World

Over the past twenty years, I have acquired a reputation in the secular world as a highly spiritual person with a "gift of healing." I have made numerous presentations and conducted healing workshops and seminars before many professional groups. I have also conducted healing sessions at spiritual retreats for men and women in the twelve-step recovery community. These workshops, seminars, and retreats have been experiential in that they combine didactic teaching with an actual healing session featuring "the laying-on of hands."

The educational component of the workshop is based on all of the material discussed in this book. The fact that God always makes his presence known in these workshops and seminars through miracles of healing is a validation of the fundamental truth of the basic thesis of the book. I will briefly describe a few of these events as a form of testimony:

> A Jewish woman, who was a self-proclaimed atheist, attended a session. She was anxious and depressed, reporting that her kidney (she only had one) was failing, and she would have to go on dialysis for the remainder of her life. When I asked her if she wanted me to pray for her kidney, she said that she was an atheist and did not believe in God. Inspired by the Holy Spirit, I replied, "You don't have to believe in God; I have enough faith for both of us." I prayed for her, and God healed her kidney.

> At a retreat for codependent women, we ended a Sunday morning workshop with a "prayer and healing circle." When the session ended, a middle-aged Irish Catholic woman would not break the circle (release the hands of the two women to either side of her). The tears were streaming down her cheeks. We had to end the session because we were about ten minutes into the breakfast hour. I gently extricated her from the circle and asked her what was wrong. She said she had suffered from asthma since she was about nine years old. As I moved around the circle and "touched her" (the Holy Spirit had directed me to position my hands over the chest area just above her heart), she felt something moving in her lungs. Suddenly, her lungs were clear and her breathing

was as easy as it had been before she had developed asthma. She feared that if the circle was broken, the condition would return. I told her that healing did not come from the circle or from me, but the healing came through the power of the Holy Ghost and from her Father, who loved her. I assured her that God was not a deceiver or a giver of false hope; the healing was real and would last.

In the early 1980s, a young Latino male attended our men's retreat. He learned that he was HIV positive. He was being treated and maintained a very healthy lifestyle, including proper dieting, nutrition, and exercise. He was a kind and gentle person who, over the years, worked through many of his life issues in recovery. Each year for twenty years, he attended our spiritual retreats. A major theme in these retreats is God's unconditional love for us and what he is committed to doing for us because of his obligations to us as a perfect Father. We speak about faith and its powers to promote miracles. And after twelve years of spiritual seeking and growing, the HIV virus disappeared from his system. God gave him a miracle of healing.

The accounts listed above are just a few of hundreds of healings that have occurred during these annual retreats for men and women in the Twelve Step recovery program.

A few years ago, I attended a substance abuse training institute in Atlanta, Georgia sponsored jointly by the National Black Alcoholism and Addiction Council (NBAAC) and Morehouse School of Medicine. The participants at the training institute were health care professionals from all over the U.S. and the West Indies. I am an adjunct professor in the institute, but this particular year, I was not scheduled to conduct a class or workshop. My plan was to relax with my old friends and enjoy the conference. But God has his own plans and purposes in all things. Through a series of coincidences, God initiated a sequence of events that placed me exactly where he had planned for me to be quite independent of whatever my plans were.

I arrived in Atlanta on the day before the training institute was scheduled to begin. The following day, I was having lunch in the hotel restaurant when a former colleague named Danielle walked in. I had not seen her for about twenty-five years. Another woman and her young son accompanied her, and I asked them to join me for lunch. We spoke about the intervening years and what had been going on in our lives. Danielle was the moderator for the opening session of the institute, which was scheduled to begin at four o'clock that afternoon. She shared with me that she had been sick with a stomach virus for the past few days and had been unable to keep solid food in her stomach.

During our lunch, her friend took the young boy to the bathroom. I asked Danielle if she would mind if I prayed for her condition. She said that she would be happy if I did. I placed my hands over her abdomen and said a brief prayer of healing. When her friend returned, we finished our lunch. Danielle did not eat, but she ordered a small fruit salad to take to her room. When we ended the lunch, she stated that she was going to her room where she would try to eat her salad and get some rest.

I did not give these events any further thought. At the appointed time, the audience was gathering in the large conference hall. There were about one hundred and twenty people in attendance. As is often the case at conferences and workshops, I was sitting in the back of the room, minding my own business, and preparing to enjoy a rare opportunity to relax and enjoy what was essentially a vacation for me.

As the speakers for the opening plenary session found their places on the dais, Danielle walked on stage, dressed in a simple black dress. She looked well as she walked to the rostrum, adjusted the microphone, and began to speak. She said, "I arrived in the hotel lobby about noon with a companion to have lunch, and I spotted my old friend, Henry. I had not seen him for about twenty-five years, and joined him for lunch." And she began to tell the story.

Immediately, my antennae went up. I had a very strong feeling that something was starting to happen that I had not planned. This institute always had a very strong spiritual orientation, and there were noted pastors and ministers in attendance. I am a low-key person who has no interest in being in the limelight. But I knew that another plan was now in play. I sank down in my seat near the back of the room and thought, "I know Danielle is not about to start the conference with this story." Because I knew within my spirit what had happened and the story she was about to tell. Notwithstanding, she went on.

"Prior to the conference, I was sick for about three or four days with a stomach virus. I did not know if I would be here or be able to stand before you and do this. But during lunch he asked me how I was doing. So I told Henry about my illness. When my friend stepped away from the table for a moment, Henry asked me if he could pray for me, and I said yes. When we finished lunch, I went to my room, ate my fruit salad, and went to sleep. I was able to keep food down for the first time in four days. I am now doing fine. He prayed for me and God answered our prayer; he healed my stomach condition." Then she said, "Henry, would you please stand so that everyone can see you." I had some very mixed feeling about all of this; however, there was more to come. So the first plenary session progressed.

There was a full five-day schedule of classes, workshops, and activities. Before the first break, an NBAAC official announced that one of the major presenters had called to say that she was unable to come. She was scheduled to conduct a workshop on Reiki, which is a form of healing based on traditional eastern medicine. The convener said that much to her regret, she had to cancel the Healing Traditions workshop unless she could find a substitute presenter. Pam, who is an old friend and NBAAC member from New York, jumped up from her seat in the front row, and very excitedly yelled, "I volunteer Henry Hudson—he will do it!"

I have learned that when God begins to reveal his intentions regarding a particular course of action for you, your best bet is to just go along with the program. So I agreed to do the three-hour workshop, which was scheduled for two o'clock the following day. I went to my room and prayed for guidance. From experience, I know when God initiates a plan, you should try not to worry about anything, just let him direct it. I had faith in God that things would work out all right.

I have some knowledge about healing methods from other cultures and traditions. In my brief outline for the workshop, I planned to talk about several historical forms of healing and their common elements. Basically, all healing is from God through the Spirit. I also know that faith in God, trust and confidence in the healer, and the belief in the possibilities of healing are the keys to successful healing. But the central focus of the workshop would be on what I knew best, which is healing in the tradition established by Christ, as best as I am able to understand what he was trying to teach.

My plan was to present the material I had put together and to end the workshop with a healing circle. In the healing circle, we simply join hands in a circle (two or more gathered in Jesus's name, touching, and agreeing). Next, I will say a brief prayer of healing asking that every request for healing be met in the name of Jesus because he said, "Whatsoever ye ask in my name, that will I do, that the Father may be glorified in the Son" (John 14:13). Then I move briefly around the circle and lay hands on the sick; "They shall lay hands on the sick and they shall recover" (Mark 16:18). Then God will do the work and accomplish what he has ordained for that particular session.

I had a lot of material to cover, and as a result, we ran over our time. I did not have enough time to do the healing circle. I informed the group we would do a special healing session later on in the conference, and anyone who was interested could attend. As I was leaving the room, a middle-aged African American woman stopped me at the door and asked me if I would pray for her. I said yes, held her hands, and said a brief prayer of healing. Although I did not know this woman and had no information about her condition, the Holy Spirit directed me to place one of my hands over her lower abdomen during the prayer. After I ended the prayer, she thanked me for my time and efforts and rushed off to her next workshop. I did not see her again during the conference.

About three weeks after I returned home, I received a telephone call from a woman who introduced herself to me and said, "You do not know me, but I am the woman who was at the conference in Atlanta and asked you to pray for me after the healing workshop." She stated that she needed to speak with me but did not know how to reach me. So she had called the NBAAC office and was able to get my office telephone number. She said that she was a nursing supervisor at one of the specialty units in a Bronx hospital. The nursing department had arranged for her to attend this conference several months in advance. But about six weeks before the conference, she had had surgery to remove a fibroid tumor.

There were complications in that the surgical incision would not heal. The seeping wound was serious enough that the bandages had to be changed three times a day. She wanted to cancel the trip. The hospital thought it was important enough for her to attend so they hired a nurse's aid to accompany her, take care of the wound, and change the dressing. She said that after I prayed for her, she continued with her schedule for that evening. When the attendant changed the dressing that night, the seepage had decreased considerably, and the wound had visibly begun to close. Before the conference ended, the seepage stopped, and the wound closed up completely. I believe that she received a miracle of healing, not by my power but by the strength of her faith that healing was possible. Something in the workshop triggered her faith. Healing was accomplished through the Holy Spirit that dwells in all of God's children.

She then asked me what church I attended and the name of my pastor. My immediate response was, "I don't do this in my church." By "this" I meant that I did not have a healing ministry in my church. But I gave her the information she had requested. My belief is that she was looking for a church with an effective healing ministry so that she could refer those in need of healing. I also believe that she wanted to be a witness that God was still in the miracle-working business.

I did not mean to imply by my response that I am the only member of my church with the gift of healing. I know that all of the children of God have the inherent ability to heal. What I was saying was that we did not have a ministry devoted specifically to healing at my church. Moreover, as I have stated previously, I don't believe that there is a church anywhere that has a reputation of being a place where anyone with any kind of sickness can go and be relatively certain of being healed. Nor have I heard of any ministers with this reputation. This includes most of the mega churches and ministries seen on television.

It stands to reason though, that if these personalities could consistently and reliably heal people of AIDS and cancer or cast out demons (heal any form of mental illness), then their lives would be as intense and busy as Jesus's life had been. Anyone with a need for healing would certainly know where these churches were located. They would certainly find their way to the healer's church to be healed.

I know that there are ministries where "believers" can go and some of them will be healed. Nevertheless, the healing is erratic and inconsistent. We see dramatic evidence of this on TV almost every day. However, what we do not see is the modern-day equivalent of lepers, outcasts, lunatics, and sinners flocking to these ministries because they know that a healer "after the order of Jesus the Christ" is there and is healing every kind of disease. There are people of faith in these congregations but there are few, if any, reliable and confident healers.

8

Healing in the Church

I have been a member of a Pentecostal church since 1986. Thus, a logical question to ask would be why I have not used these healing gifts in the church in a more formal way. The answer is related to realities about church doctrines, traditions, beliefs, and practices. It is important to remember that every church is under the authority of religious beliefs based on a particular theological doctrine. The underlying theology forming the basis for the religious practice will determine how God is understood by the congregation, and how God and the Holy Spirit will be allowed to manifest in the church and in the lives of its members.

Prevailing Christian theology suggests that creative power does not reside in the sons and daughters God created in his own image and likeness. Contrary to what Jesus taught us, we still believe that access to our natural heritage is gained through mastery of complex theologies, ideologies, and belief systems. Every religious group has its rituals of salvation and the signs that indicate mastery. In Pentecostalism, for example, you must seek the Holy Ghost to be saved, and you must speak in other tongues to prove that you have received it. However, if you have not spoken in tongues, the believers assume that you do not have an anointing of the Holy Ghost in your life or your work.

The Bible declares that we are created in God's own image and likeness (Gen. 1:27) and that the breath of life (Gen. 2:7) animates us. This is the same Spirit that was the active force in the creation of the universe (Gen. 1:2). What this means is that as sons and daughters of God, we are endowed with the creative power of the Holy Spirit by our Father God, including power over sickness. Jesus reaffirms this truth when he said we shall do greater works than the works (miracles and healing) he did (John 14:12), if we believed what he was teaching us, and followed his instructions and examples.

However, many Christians do not believe what Jesus said about his divinity or what he said about ours. Our persistent denial of the divinity of Jesus makes it impossible for us to entertain the possibility of own divine nature. Jesus defined this tendency to deny the reality of divinity in him and in all of God's children as unbelief. The scripture illustrates the potency of doubt and unbelief and their influence on healing by reporting that when Jesus returned to Nazareth, "He did not many mighty works there because of their unbelief" (Matt. 13:58). The people knew Jesus as Joseph's son; thus, he could not literally be the son of God. The source of their unbelief was doubts about Jesus's divinity.

Our doubts about Jesus's divinity and our confusion about God's true nature are based on the tendencies of all Christians, including the disciples, to misunderstand what Jesus taught about himself, about God our perfect Father, and about who we are. I have never "spoken in tongues" nor have I been "carried away in the Spirit." Nevertheless, I know that I have an anointing for healing, based on what Jesus has taught us. He said that anything he did, we can do! Of myself, I can do nothing, but through the power of God within (Christ Jesus) I can do all things—including healing the sick!

Jesus said that I am a worthy child of God. Therefore, I am entitled to have anything I need from God and can get it by simply asking and believing. I had the ability to inspire miracles of healing before I came to the church. Since joining the church, this gift has been enhanced because I asked God to grant me more power to do the works that he had assigned to me. Circumstances and events in the world during this period required more power to comfort and heal than I believed I possessed.

In the mideighties, there was a full-blown medical crisis associated with the onset of the AIDS epidemic. In my work with hospital employees, there were several clients in my caseload who were HIV-positive or who had spouses, relatives, or friends with this disease. During this period, anyone afflicted with this disease had no hope. They were outcast in the same sense as the lepers of Jesus's time. At the altar, I ask God to give me what was needed to help his children who were offered no hope by the world. I ask for no other gifts of the Spirit other than the ability to be a better healer and comforter. And I ask, believing. I will now share with you a couple of stories about healing in the church that will demonstrate this point.

During my second year in the church, the leader of the Women's Department asked my brother and me to prepare the dinner for the annual Women's Day. It was a busy day, so we did not finish cleaning the kitchen until the afternoon service was almost completed. When I went up to the main sanctuary, the last of four speakers was about to make her presentation.

She approached the rostrum walking with a cane and began her message by telling us that during the previous week, she suffered a serious back injury in a car accident. Initially, she did not think she was going to be able to drive from Connecticut for the service because of her injury, but by the grace of God, she was able to make it. She shared with the congregation that she was in considerable pain and had to be very careful of her movements. Then she began to speak.

She made a good presentation, but I missed most of the message. While listening to her presentation as I sat in the back of the church, the Holy Spirit said, "You ought to go pray for her after the service." I went back and forth in my mind about this and reluctantly stood in the back of the line of people who were waiting to speak with her after the service. I was hesitant about following the direction of the Spirit because I am familiar with church life.

I was a relatively new member of the church, and I was uncertain about how an evangelist would respond to a spontaneous offer of healing by someone she did not know. Sick people in churches are usually uncomfortable with anyone doing anything of a spiritual nature for them other than the pastor, someone in the congregation with some status, or someone whose gifts are known to them. I also had questions about my abilities to heal in a church environment. Because I was a relatively new born-again Christian, I felt that it would seem pushy and presumptuous of me to offer this gift to anyone in the church. But being obedient to the voice of the Holy Spirit, I pressed ahead and took the risk!

When I reached her, I simply said, "I enjoyed your presentation. Would you like for me to pray for your back?" She looked a little surprised, but then said yes. I held her by one hand and gently and carefully laid my other hand on the small of her back. I said a very brief prayer of healing and said, "God is going to bless you." She thanked me for my prayer, and I went about my business for that day. I also forgot about the event.

Two Sundays later, one of the older saints approached me and said, "I want to thank you for what you did for my cousin." Of course, I had no idea what she was talking about. She told me that the evangelist for whom I prayed on Women's Day, was her cousin. The cousin called her on Friday the following week and told her that at the end of the service, a man had suddenly "popped up" in front of her, introduced himself, and gave her a compliment on her message. He then asked if he could pray for her back. She stated that she was surprised but said yes. A couple of days later, the pain was gone, and she could walk without the cane. God had given her a miracle of healing in the church by a stranger.

I believe that God sent me to my church to do counseling and healing. However, I have been asked to do many other things in the church other than what I believe I have been called to do. Although I have done them to the best of my abilities, I cannot do any of them as well as I do counseling, teaching, and healing. They are not what God has ordained me to do and are not related to my true calling or my anointing.

Here is the dilemma: it is obvious to some in the church family that God has given me healing gifts. However, because I have not demonstrated any of the agreed-upon signs that I have the Holy Ghost, there are doubts about whether I am saved and have a true anointing from God. Let me make one thing clear: I know my pastor has faith, trust, and confidence in me. As a matter of fact, several years ago he stopped me in the vestibule of the church and asked me to pray for him after a Sunday service prior to his leaving for the annual COGIC convocation. I did not know at the time that he been diagnosed with lung cancer. I laid hands on his chest and said a brief prayer requesting healing and strength. He went to the convocation and through much prayer and fasting; he eventually received a total healing by the prayers of the saints and his faith in God.

Nevertheless, I believe that there is an expectation in the church that until I get carried away in the Spirit and shout, fall out, run around the church, or speak in tongues, they will not accept that I have the Holy Ghost or a true anointing. Many traditional Christians also believe this with great certainty. Unless the agreed-upon signs are shown, there is no evidence of the Holy Ghost. Therefore, no anointing! According to them, I could never be a true, born-again Christian with any of the gifts of the Holy Spirit unless I spoke in other tongues (1 Cor. 12:1–11).

In fact, an elderly church mother, who is a longtime family friend, has commented that I may be able to do these things in the secular world but I do not do them "under the anointing." She is suggesting that I am able to do miracles of healing, but they are coming from some natural source rather than from God by the Holy Spirit. But what she is really saying is that I do not behave like a typical Pentecostal; I do not profess to know how other people should live their lives or how they should behave in the world in terms of standards of behavior and moral codes. Furthermore, I try to be kind, tolerant, patient, and nonjudgmental. I happen to believe that God loves all of his children equally, including homosexuals, atheists, drug addicts, alcoholics, and others whose behavior we would define as sinful. I also happen to believe that God's love for his children is unconditional; thus they are entitled to healing whether they are "saved" or not. Above all else, I know that I am not the appointed judge.

Another problem is that I am not ritualistic in my church attendance. I rarely fast, attend prayer services, or attend weekday worship services. I have never attended Bible studies because these studies are mostly about theology and doctrine. It is not that I believe that I am above all of this. It is just that as one who is trying to be a true Christian, I try to follow Jesus's teaching and instruction in all things. Jesus spoke about ritualistic prayer and warned against vain repetitions in his instructions on appropriate methods of prayer (Matt. 6:6–13). He also told us that the only form of true worship is "in spirit and in truth" (John 4:24).

Moreover, I believe that how Christians behave in their daily lives and in their interactions with each other is a better indication of their commitment to follow Jesus than anything they may say or do in a church service. A final point is that I am almost seventy years old, and I have been blessed to be able to continue working full-time at my true calling (therapist, healer). I believe true worship is doing the work of God in all of our daily activities. Jesus illustrates this requirement beautifully when he told us, "Let your light so shine before men, that they may see your good works, and glorify your Father which is in heaven" (Matt. 5:16).

Therefore, according to many of my church brothers and sisters, I am probably not truly "saved and sanctified" and consequently teach and heal through some natural means rather than through the power of the Holy Ghost. It seems to me Jesus already resolved this issue when he was accused of healing through something other than the power of God (Luke 11:14–26). These accusations against Jesus were also based on the belief that Jesus was a heretic because he did not have the proper reverence for religious doctrine and ritual and because of his relationships with Samaritans.

The irony is that in most churches, ministers, evangelists, elders, and other church leaders who should be routinely doing the "greater works" are not doing miracles of healing. Most have passed the "tests of holiness" in that they speak in tongues, are carried away in the Spirit, and regularly do their holy dances during services. According to church doctrine, they are all under the anointing and presumably have formal sanctum to heal in the church. There is hardly any evidence, however, that any of them other than the pastor can consistently do the greater works of healing. And above all else, there is almost never a service devoted strictly to healing.

In many modern churches, there is a ministry of music, an outreach ministry, a missions department, a tract ministry, a foreign mission, and a ministry related to all of the things that are part of the church's mission and deemed essential to church family life. Our church does not have a ministry devoted specifically to healing the sick; the majority of your churches do not have one either! Furthermore, I have not heard it "rumored about" that there is a church anywhere in the New York metropolitan area where someone can go and be healed. I doubt there is a church of this nature in your community either.

We can account for this failure of the modern church to make formal provision within its organizational structure for healing the sick because its theology minimizes the importance of healing in our Christian ministries. Another factor is that we do not believe we are capable of doing miracles of healing because we seldom see them done in the church with any degree of consistency.

In my eighteen years in the church, I have been very careful not to pursue a personal agenda by going through the motions of gaining mastery over the necessary doctrines or rituals in an attempt to gain status in the church. Many have followed this path. However, once they have achieved the desired status or position, they leave the church to pursue their own agenda. I could have followed this path and achieved the status of minister or evangelist, and with the title, I would have been able to establish my own healing ministry or church based on my beliefs and "special gifts." Although this is common in church history, my belief is that the gift of healing is not special—it's a potential in every Christian.

My dilemma has always been whether it would be possible to develop a healing ministry in the church based on the model developed by Jesus in accordance with his instructions. If it is possible to integrate healing into a traditional church structure, then a much larger purpose will have been served by my being in a church. However, if the barriers of theology and doctrine cannot be breached, I believe God will open other paths for developing successful healing structures in the world that are based on Jesus's instructions and example.

Let me give you a prime example of how commitment to theology and doctrinal ideologies hinder the basic messages of Jesus's teaching about who we are and how God regards us. Although the events described below happen to involve a Catholic church, the commitment to theology and doctrine is typical of all churches.

I once attended a healing service in a Catholic church near my home. The healing service is held one Saturday each month but is not a formal element in this church's organizational structure. I attended the services with a good friend who is Catholic. The service features the laying-on of hands. Very often, people will collapse at the touch of the healers so it is common to have designated catchers. When they asked for volunteers, I agreed to serve with my friend.

At the end of the service, Holy Communion was served. I was standing in line prepared to take Communion because I knew that I was worthy. I am Christian, and I had reason to believe that I was in good standing with God. Much to my surprise, the priest announced that only Catholics in the audience were eligible to receive Holy Communion. I was embarrassed that I wasn't eligible to take Communion because I was not a member of an organization based on a theology never mentioned in the Bible and a doctrine not practiced by our collective Savior who was a rabbi in Judaism. Perhaps, I was naïve or ignorant in not remembering that doctrine rules. I got caught up in the moment and was not thinking parochially. The message communicated to me was that I was not a true follower of Christ because I do not follow the theology, doctrines, and beliefs of the Catholic church.

Even though I had the same anointing from God as the priest, I would never be permitted to manifest healing in that setting because I did not follow Catholic dogma! The message was clear: I was not Catholic and was unworthy of the sacraments. The Apostles' Doctrine in the Bible suggested that a probable consequence of the unworthy participation in Holy Communion could be sickness, death, or some other severe punishment for offending God. Many Catholics and Protestants believe this to be true because it is written in the Bible and they believe every word of the Bible is true (I Cor. 11:24–30).

Christians continue to preach this message despite the fact that we have no actual proof that God operates in this manner. For example, we did not hear of any increase in mortality rates among Catholic priests who sexually abused children or among the ranks of the church authorities who covered for them. Unless they gave up participation in Communion or openly repented, they all should have perished according to this scripture. The reality is that God does not kill his wayward children for disobedience, although we continue to suggest this in our theologies and our sermons.

Many Catholics have been directed to me and received healing, but according to Catholic dogma, I am not properly saved and will probably die and go to hell. Then again, Jesus wouldn't be permitted to do healing in that church because he wasn't Catholic either—he was Jewish. This is a good example of how a modern-day religion continues to miss Jesus's primary message.

Another example is related to an incident during an interfaith service held in New York City in the aftermath of the 9/11 attack on the World Trade Center. A minister belonging to a mainstream Protestant denomination participated in a memorial service in Yankee Stadium. He offered a prayer and remarks, as did every religious leader that day. However, because he failed to follow the doctrine of his church as it relates to issuing a call for repentance, he was suspended from the ministry. Furthermore, according to the doctrine of this church, sharing the dais with those having different religious beliefs was an act of heresy. He was later reinstated, but this type of misinterpretation of Jesus's basic message for love, compassion, and tolerance is typical of most religious denominations.

9

Good News versus Theology and Doctrine

The essence of the gospel Jesus brought to the world is fully captured in the fourteenth chapter of the Gospel of John. It begins with some of the most important words spoken by Christ. Jesus is reminding us that there is absolutely nothing we should be worried about in this physical life or the life afterward. He encouraged us by saying "Let not your heart be troubled: ye believe in God, believe also in me. In my Father's house there are many mansions: if it were not so, I would have told you. I go to prepare a place for you, And if I go and prepare a place for you, I will come again, and receive you unto myself; that where I am, there ye may be also" (John 14:1–3).

In this report, Jesus again addressed the issues of his divinity and the true nature and character of God. When Philip asked him to reveal the true nature of God, Jesus asked the disciples and modern-day Christians a direct and simple question: "Have I been so long time with you, and yet hast thou not known me, Philip? He that hath seen me hath seen the Father; and how saith thou then, Shew us the Father?" (John 14:9). Thus, the good news, according to our Lord and Savior, is that we can know exactly who God is by simply understanding who Jesus was during his life and ministry in the physical realm!

According to Jesus, God is not the fearful, sectarian God of the Old Testament but the perfect Father of all humanity. Through his ministry of healing Jesus demonstrated that God loves all of humanity unconditionally. By clearly defining himself and God as one, Jesus gives us all of the truth in the gospel of Jesus Christ that we will ever need. God, whom we have not seen, has the same temperament and character as Jesus. Therefore Jesus's character and nature are the model for our spiritual development. Moreover, through his example in the world, Jesus has shown the unlimited possibilities for all of God's children to evolve into spiritual maturity. Thus, manifesting the ability to do the greater works of healing has to be the goal of every Christian and an essential element in the life and purpose of the church.

It is very difficult for us to understand the full power and drama of healing miracles and the potential impact they have on all who witness them. However, the following report is a good example:

> "And as Jesus passed by, he saw a man which was born blind from his birth. And his disciples asked him saying, Master, who did sin, this man, or his parents, that he was born blind?" Jesus answered, "Neither hath this man sinned, nor his parents: but that the works of God should be made manifest in him. I must work the works of him that sent me, while it is day: the night cometh, when no man can work. As long as I am in the world, I am the light of the world." When he had thus spoken, he spat on the ground, and made clay of the spittle, and he anointed the eyes of the blind man with the clay, And said unto him, "Go, wash in the pool of Siloam." He went his way therefore, and washed, and came seeing" (John 9:1–7).

The man, who knew nothing about Jesus, followed his instructions, and "came seeing." Jesus's dramatic manifestation of the power of God caused a great disturbance among the people. As the rest of the ninth chapter of the Gospel of John indicates, the neighbors were excited but disbelieving, and the scribes and Pharisees were upset and very angry. Everyone found it very difficult to believe that a man who was born blind could regain his sight and so they argued about how this could be. We know that the same levels of excitement, joy, confusion, and disbelief were surely generated whenever Jesus healed a leper or called a dead person back to life.

All of Jesus's works were powerful statements that God is very near and his healing power can be "accessed" by anyone. I am suggesting that Jesus's dramatic acts of healing were primarily a means of gaining the world's attention. Jesus was proclaiming by his works that something powerful and unusual was occurring. It was a declaration that "the kingdom of God has come nigh unto you" (Luke 10:9). Although the Gospel of Jesus Christ has been seriously distorted, misinterpreted and misunderstood, we are fortunate that the records of his healing ministry are still there for us to observe and understand.

I believe that it is essential to elevate healing to a place of prominence in the Christian church. To do this successfully, we must make healing an important aspect of our mission and purpose. We must give healing the sick the same degree of importance in our overall ministry as Jesus gave it. We will not be able to do this unless we can transcend the complexities of our own theologies, ideologies, and doctrines and begin to know the truth. If a religious theology or doctrine is based on scriptural elements that conflict with Jesus's teachings, that conflict must be resolved. To do this successfully, we must decide if we will follow the gospel of Jesus Christ or follow the teaching of other biblical authorities and the subsequent doctrines that have evolved from their diverse teachings.

Let me give another example of what I mean by the message versus doctrine dilemma. A man addicted to heroin and alcohol came to our church from the Addicts Rehabilitation Center (ARC), a local drug treatment program in the Harlem community. He was the son of a bishop in COGIC and was very committed to his addictions. This man taught all of the members of my church a powerful lesson about God's unconditional love and the faithfulness of our pastor as a true follower of Christ. He took the church on a long and painful journey before he was healed. In addition to his drug problems, he suffered from ulcers on his legs that would not heal. His journey ultimately took him to a hospital that specializes in the long-term treatment of individuals with chronic diseases.

During this time, he attended a Communion and foot-washing service on New Year's Eve. During the foot washing, I noticed that he had large sores on his legs—a legacy from his active drug use and one of the reasons he was in the long-term care facility. He had them for years and modern medicine could not heal them. So, I prayed for the ulcers. After a short time, the ulcers healed. In the hospital, he got his addiction under control through the AA program. Through much prayer and many miracles, he was eventually discharged—whole and healed—from a hospital to which he had been sent to die.

He returned to his church roots and is now a pastor in his father's church in Detroit. He visits our church in New York to preach from time to time. The heart of the message in his testimony and his sermons is how God saved him from his sins of addiction and a life of active drug abuse. But in the telling of his story, he seldom speaks of the miracle of healing of his crippling ulcers and the miracle of his recovery through the AA fellowship. One must ask whether the testimony of this addict-turned-pastor would be more meaningful to congregants seeking recovery if they were led to the tangible doorsteps of an AA meeting on their way to the intangible street of salvation.

I am not claiming that my specific prayer was the catalyst that precipitated his healing. The pastor and most of the congregation frequently prayed for his deliverance during the three or four years he was involved with the church. The point is that God performed a miracle of healing on his leg but the major focus is that he "returned to Christ." The value of the gift of AA to the world as a path for the healing of addictions is continually denigrated in many of our churches, even though AA history recognizes that it is a "God-given program." It is also evident that AA operates more in the "spirit of Christ" than most of our churches. Although he sometimes refers to me as his "sponsor" in his sermons, he never mentions AA as a major factor in his healing.

His miracle of healing from the crippling ulcers on his legs, which the medical profession was powerless to heal, also is not part of his testimony. His primary message is that getting "saved and sanctified" is the key to entering into the kingdom of God. Jesus never said that our theologies, doctrines, belief systems, or rituals are indications that "the kingdom of God is come nigh unto you" (Luke 10:9). But in the Gospel of Luke, he said to the seventy that miracles of healing are the message. So we continue to miss an important message.

In church doctrine, we tend to minimize the value and importance of "good works," and healing is a prime example. You have heard it many times, and we believe it to be true: the apostle Paul said, "For by grace are ye saved through faith; and not of yourselves: it is the gift of God: Not of works, lest any man should boast" (Eph. 2:8–9). Now, what Paul has said may be totally true, only partially true, or be false (I believe that the statement is false because Jesus said "Let your light so shine before men that they may see your good works, and glorify your Father which is in heaven" (Matt. 5:16).

Paul, however, is not the ultimate authority on God or his kingdom. Jesus spoke to Paul in a vision, but there is no record that Paul actually saw God. Therefore his knowledge of God and the kingdom is limited at best. Jesus is the only authority on God because he is the only one who has seen God. In fact, John identified Jesus as the "Word made flesh" (John 1:14). Because he is God's only *Word* made flesh and manifested into the physical world, Jesus is God's true spokesman. Therefore, Jesus is the ultimate authority on God and the kingdom.

I believe Jesus is saying that healing the sick is a good and necessary work; it is one sure sign that God is come near unto us. Therefore, if people knew with certainty that reliable healing was available in our churches, they will know that God is nigh and can be touched by any of us. They will also know that it is possible to establish a strong relationship with him because God is not in a far-off place, waiting for them to die in their sins so that he can torment them in eternal fire. If the mission of the church is to bring souls to Christ, there is no better way to do this than to follow Jesus's example of healing the sick and his teaching of the true gospel as it concerns our perfect Father. What other reason might God have had for sending his son to us in the first place?

Thus, like the unnamed man characterized by the disciples as one who "followeth us not" (Mark 9:38), I have done miracles of healing and cast out demons through the healing of mental illnesses with long-and short-term, Christ-based therapy. I have done this regularly in the secular world, but I have done very little formal healing in the church. In fact, even if there is a specific altar call for healing, I am unable to participate. I am usually in the finance office counting money as a part of my duties as a Finance Committee member. However, I am certain that if my church had a healing ministry, I would have a role in this ministry because healing is my calling.

I believe that another problem with healing in the church is our single-minded commitment to our traditional religious theology. For the most part, this is based on the Old Testament, the teachings of the apostle Paul, and the Apostles' Doctrine described in Acts. It is evident that we have given every speaker and writer in the Bible equal status to Jesus as authorities on God and God's kingdom. The ratio of sermons based on what spokesmen from the Old Testament and the Acts of the Apostles have to say about God and the kingdom versus those focusing exclusively on what Jesus said is enormously tilted in favor of these other authorities. Every Sunday, we hear much more about what Paul, David, Joshua, Samuel, Isaiah, or Jeremiah said about God and the kingdom of heaven than what Jesus said about God, salvation, and the kingdom of God.

We consistently hear about what Jesus did for us rather than what he was trying to teach us. Every Sunday, what we generally hear about Christ is that Jesus died on the cross for your sins (feel guilty, repent)! The reason for this imbalance is that we tend to teach a theology based on the reports in the Old Testament, the law, the Apostles' Doctrine, and Paul's epistles rather than on the truth about God as Jesus taught and demonstrated.

Fear is a sure sign that the children of God have forgotten who they are, and more importantly, have forgotten to whom they belong. If we truly knew that God is our perfect Father, as Jesus told us, and that his love for us is unconditional and unchanging, then we would truly be able to "fear not." Assuredly, we would not be fearful of sickness, disease, or even death! Before Jesus called Lazarus from the grave, he said to Martha, "I am the resurrection, and the life: he that believeth in me, though he were dead, yet shall he live: And whosoever liveth and believeth in me shall never die. Believeth thou this?" (John 11:25–26).

The presence of fear and anxiety are also a sign that we have not paid sufficient attention to Jesus's words to us or that we do not believe what he has said. We are fearful of sickness and diseases. We are fearful of death also because we have been taught to fear our perfect Father who loves us unconditionally. Fear of God was not the good news Jesus brought us. Jesus gave us all of the assurance we should ever need when he said, "Let not your heart be troubled: ye believe in God, believe also in me" (John 14:1). He also made a pledge of peace and security when he said, "Peace I leave you, my peace I give unto you. Let not your heart be troubled, neither let it be afraid" (John 14:27).

He left his peace with us along with the promise of another "Comforter" who would abide with us forever (John 14:16–21). The Comforter, in the form of the Holy Ghost, has returned to the world after a long absence. Nevertheless, a large segment of the Christian world continues to operate in the spirit of the Apostles' Doctrine in service to the God of Abraham, Isaac, and Jacob. To do the greater works, we need to look at the way we use Jesus and his teachings in our religious doctrines and theologies. It is also imperative that we understand the full implications of what we are teaching in our messages. Let me now share with you a story which will demonstrate the point I am making.

On a recent Sunday, we had a wonderful message from a visiting pastor from Cleveland. His theme was "*The Storms Keep on Coming*". His message was based on the Apostle Paul's experience of a great storm. Paul reported that after the ship had been driven by the storm for several days, the captain and the crew had made the decision to abandon the ship. According to the spokesmen in this account on the severity of the storm: "And when neither sun nor stars in many days appeared, and no small tempest lay on us, all hope that we should be saved was then taken away" (Acts 27:20).

This fine preacher then spoke about how Job survived his storm and how Jonah endured his storm. He also spoke about Peter's experience when he attempted to walk out to Jesus on the storm-tossed sea. The main thrust of the overall message was that we can depend on God to see us through our storms. This is, of course, a valid point to make. Oddly enough though, this inspiring pastor never told the story about Jesus, the master of the storms and the waves, who gave us a different solution to the problems of storms:

> "And when they had sent away the multitude, they took him even as he was in the ship. And there were also with him other little ships. And there arose a great storm of wind, and the waves beat into the ship, so that it was now full. And he was in the hinder part of the ship, asleep on a pillow: and they awake him, and say unto him, 'Master, carest thou not that we perish?' And he arose, and rebuked the wind, and said unto the sea, 'Peace, be still.' And the wind ceased, and there was a great calm. And he said unto them, 'Why are ye so fearful? How is it that ye have no faith?'" (Mark 4:36–40).

Jesus wanted the disciples to understand they should not be fearful of anything when they were with him. How could they fear the wrath of a storm, knowing that Jesus was in the boat? Jesus taught us that we have the power to do anything he was able to do. If the apostle Paul truly understood Jesus's teaching, neither he nor the others on the boat would have been "terrorized" for three days by a storm no matter how great the tempest. Under the "greater works" principle, we have the power to "speak to our storms," and with faith, they will cease. It stands to reason that if Paul believed and did not doubt, he could have calmed the sea and the storms with a simple command of *Peace, be still!*

Jesus demonstrated in his ministry that it did not matter the severity of the storm. We have the power to handle it! But this very good preacher gave us a subtly different message that day. He was saying that if we pray fervently enough, the God of Abraham, Isaac, and Jacob may eventually hear our prayer and deliver us. *It took, however, three days, a visit from an angel, and a shipwreck before Paul and the sailors were delivered!*

Paul is venerated by Christians who stand in awe of his Holy Ghost experience. The thought in the modern-day Christian's mind, whose righteousness we must remember has been defined as "filthy rags," would surely doubt his or her ability to calm their life storms based on what we teach them. If Paul and the disciples did not demonstrate the ability to manifest "mountain moving faith" or to consistently do the greater works, then the average Christian will have doubts about their abilities to do them. The question I would ask is, if Jesus's disciples did not literally believe what he tried to teach them, what hope is there for us to learn?

This pastor then shared with the congregation a personal story about how God had given him a miracle of healing from colon cancer. He ended his sermon with a call for repentance. He then made a second call for healing. I believe that about three times as many people responded to the healing call than to the call for repentance. But the major focus of his message was on sin and repentance rather than God's unconditional love for us. Thus, by its focus, the message generated subtle doubt and unbelief by generating questions in the minds of the sick in the congregation about the state of their holiness; and whether they deserved anything for God because of sin. The basic message according to this pastor was that your perfect Father's love and protection is available to you but first, you must repent. In the ritual of repentance, you must "confess your sins and profess the Lord Jesus with your mouth and be saved." Then you may be healed.

I do not believe that any great works of healing were done that Sunday because of the doubts and unbelief generated in the minds of those in the congregation needing a miracle of healing. I have not heard of any recent miracles of healing in the church related to that sermon. Thus, we continue to do business as usual and pain and suffering continue in the world. If we had faith in God who loves us unconditionally and truly believed Jesus's teachings, we would be doing the "greater works" routinely.

The final problem we have in providing miracles of healing in the church is related to the persistent problems of the "doubting legacy" the disciples have passed down to the church. We have trouble believing that we can do real miracles of healing. We have doubts about how God truly feels about us: does he love us unconditionally or are we unclean in his sight? Furthermore, if we believe that the most important thing about our "unsaved" or "nonbeliever" brothers and sisters is that they need to accept our beliefs and doctrines (repent) before they can have what they need from God, then we will doubt whether they deserve a miracle of healing from their perfect Father until they do as we say. It is also difficult for us to believe that this whole process of getting what we need from God could be as simple as Jesus has instructed us. "Ask believing and you shall receive" (Matt. 21:2) is not complicated enough for the average human being who happens to be Christian.

A few years ago, I conducted a five-hour class called Basic Principles of Christian Healing at an NBAAC Training Institute in Atlanta, Georgia. In this class, there were about twenty participants from different sections of the country, including several pastors. The content was based on much of the material contained in this book. I assured the class that every assertion I made about healing and its proper place in the gospel was based on Jesus's words. I reminded the "students" that I had not created or "made up" any of the information I was giving them. I also emphasized that everything I told them about God's true nature and our relationship with him was based on Jesus's gospel and not on my own teachings.

Strangely enough, they could not accept the good news Jesus brought us about God and repent of their confusion and misunderstandings. They continually refuted all of my positions and assertions, based on something that Paul, one of the disciples, or a spokesman from the Old Testament had said. I was constantly reminded of what someone else other than Jesus said about the issues under discussion. Their responses to me suggested a total commitment to theology and doctrine. Moreover, their strong and fervent commitment to their doctrinal beliefs was based on the theological fallacy that every word in the Bible is the unalterable word of God and that every word is true. It is odd that we continue to believe this despite what we know about the history of the Bible and the tendencies of human beings to distort facts and exaggerate.

According to the apostle John, Jesus was God's Word made flesh. He also suggested that Jesus was the only true source of information about God's character and nature. John said, "And the Word was made flesh, and dwelt among us, (and we beheld his glory, the glory as of the only begotten of the Father) full of grace and truth" (John 1:14).

The experience in this class also served as a classic example of how deeply ingrained in the Christian personality system is the belief that every voice in the Bible carries equal weight and authority. The thesis of inerrancy is a false belief. I make this statement boldly based on what Jesus himself had to say about this issue, so do not brand me as a heretic or blasphemer. The idea is not something I thought or made up; Jesus said it! "My doctrine is not mine, but His that sent me" (John 7:16). Jesus speaks for God! Therefore, any spokesman in the Bible whose statements or positions are not in accordance with what Jesus said is in error.

I made one recommendation to them about healing. I suggested that they reverse the order of their altar calls and make a general call for healing before they made the call for repentance. But they were committed to their doctrines and their ways! If they had been open to my basic thesis about the importance of healing in Christian ministry, I would have made the following suggestion. In the altar call for healing, simply say to the sick and infirm in your congregation, "Your Father in heaven is a perfect father who loves you unconditionally. Jesus, who is one with God, told us that whatsoever we ask the Father in his name, he will do it. If there is anyone in the sanctuary who needs a miracle of healing from any sickness or disease, or deliverance from any life condition or situation, come! Come to the altar and be healed! Come as the woman with the issue of blood came. She came thinking, 'If I can just get close enough to Jesus to touch the hem of his garment, I know I will be healed.' Come believing! Come as the centurion came, who said, 'If you but speak the word, I know my servant will be healed.' Come believing with me, that God, your perfect father, is a healer. And you will be healed! Then, boldly walk out among them, and act on those powerful words spoken by Jesus that 'They shall lay hands on the sick and they shall recover'" (Mark 16:18).

I knew that if they truly believed the word of God (Jesus), they would be able to "Say unto them, the kingdom of God is come nigh unto you" (Luke 10:9). If they had been willing to take this step of faith, then all would see the truth of Jesus's words, because miracles of healing and deliverance will occur Sunday after Sunday. Nonetheless, they could not give up their doctrinal beliefs in the truth of every word in the Bible nor would they give up their beliefs that their pastoral purpose and Christian obligations are to win souls for Christ through their sermons and exultation rather than by manifesting the power of God and his love as Jesus did through miracles of healing. There was no evidence that they believed me or were willing to act on my recommendations. They have not repented and believed the gospel as Jesus admonished us to do!

The apostle John has already spoken about these human tendencies. Speaking about Jesus, the Word made flesh, John said early on that "In him was life; and the life was the light of men. And the light shineth in darkness; and the darkness comprehended it not" (John 1:4–5). *I truly believe that our theologies and doctrines are a hindrance to our ability to comprehend the true gospel of Jesus Christ, and as a result, much of Christianity continues to dwell in darkness.* We will never be able to correct this flaw in our perception until we recognize that Jesus is the only authority in the Bible as it relates to the true nature of God and God's plan and purpose for humanity.

10

Missing the Message

For the most part, the disciples misunderstood what Jesus was trying to teach them about the true nature of God. Because confidence in God is a necessary condition for consistent healing, the Christian healer must resolve these contradictions in Christian theology about God's true nature. The essences of the contradiction revolves around the unresolved question of whether our heavenly Father is a God of fear as he has been portrayed in the Old Testament or the God of love as Jesus manifested him. It is very difficult to have confidence and faith simultaneously in a God of fear and a God of love.

Jesus defined and manifested God as a perfect father with the following basic characteristics: unconditional love for all of his children, infinite compassion, infinite patience, tolerance, dependable provider, nonjudgmental attitude, and a generous forgiver of all transgressions.

On the other hand, we have the God of Abraham, Isaac, and Jacob. The God of the Old Testament has very different characteristics than the perfect Father of whom Jesus speaks. He is a God who has a chosen people; he plays favorites with his children. He agrees that his chosen people have enemies who deserve death and destruction. The God of the Old Testament, according to the record, will aid you in the destruction of your enemies, and under certain circumstances, will mandate that you kill them all, including their women, children, and animals. Furthermore, he will help you destroy them to prove that he is your God and you are his chosen people. In other words, he is a God with an ego similar to human egos with something to prove.

The God of the Old Testament gave Moses ten commandments from which thousands of laws and rules of behavior have evolved. The priest and religious authorities taught the people that you must remember and obey all of the laws, rules and regulations or God will take offence and do horrible things to you. For example, this God permitted the prophet Elisha to call forth two she bears and tear apart forty-two children who mocked him (2 Kings 2:23–24). Elisha learned from his mentor, Elijah, that the power of God was available to destroy anyone who displeases you or God. Elijah was known for calling down fire from heaven on his enemies, something the God of Abraham, Isaac, and Jacob apparently sanctioned (2 Kings 1:9–13).

He is a God who required that woman and children subjugate themselves to the rule of men, many of whom were not mature or mentally balanced enough to hold power over the lives of other human beings. This is the God of Abraham, Isaac, and Jacob, who permitted the supposed descendents of Noah's good sons, Shem and Japheth (theologically defined as the father of the Europeans), to enslave and do horrible things for generations to the supposed descendents of Ham (African, Arabs, and other people of color). Ham was cursed by his father Noah for inadvertently looking on his nakedness following Noah's drunken sleep (Gen. 9:22–26). The God of Abraham, Isaac, and Jacob is also the one who instructed Moses that the operative law governing relationships between God's children was "An eye for an eye and a tooth for a tooth" (Lev. 24:20).

It would be a real stretch of the logical mind to think about Jesus or the God Jesus represented doing any of the horrible things that this God did to his children or permitted his children to do to each other. We have to accept that all human beings are God's children unless Satan is listed somewhere as a cocreator with God. Moreover, if we accept that all human beings are children of God, then we are obligated to truly love one another as Jesus has said. We must love our neighbors (those with whom we are close and familiar) and love our enemies (those who are different and whom we believe that we have reasons to fear). We certainly must love everyone who falls in between these two extremes.

These conflicting images of God, who according to the word is "an unchanging God" (Heb. 13:8), create a high level of confusion in the minds of his children. It is very difficult to love and trust a father who has extremely violent tendencies, is unpredictable, and gives preferential treatment. Even the disciples had great difficulty understanding Jesus's conceptualizations of God. When Jesus said, "He that hath seen me, hath seen the Father" (John 14:9), they still did not understand. Because of our reliance on their teaching and example, neither have we.

We know that the twelve disciples did not comprehend Jesus's basic teaching because of some of the things they did and said. Several Bible stories suggest that they were as concerned about worldly things as today's Christians. Some were as preoccupied with status, power, prestige, and position as many in our churches today. They were also prejudiced against other human beings, mainly Samaritans and heathens. It is also apparent that many Christians today have not mastered Jesus's basic commandment to "love one another as I have loved you" (John

15:12). Unloving thoughts and behaviors toward people who are different, of course, are contrary to what Jesus taught but quite faithful to the Old Testament teachings.

The disciples' concerns about rank and status are clearly revealed in the question posed to Jesus concerning which of them would occupy the seat of power (at Jesus's right hand) in heaven. They also did not understand the truth of what Jesus was trying to teach us about the high and equal regard God has for all of his children. None of us is more or less valued than the other in God's sight and none of us are more or less loved than the others. We are all children of God, and he loves us equally. This is one of the fundamental differences between the God of the Old Testament and God as Jesus represented him.

The prophets of the Old Testament were quick to visit the wrath of God on those who offended them. Like the prophets of old, the disciples continued to believe in the God of their fathers, who would do terrible things to people who displeased or disrespected him. The story from the Gospel of Luke provides a good illustration of this point:

> "And it came to pass, when the time was come that he should be received up, he stedfastly set his face to go to Jerusalem, and sent messengers before his face: and they went, and entered into a village of the Samaritans, to make ready for him. And they did not receive him, because his face was as though he would go to Jerusalem. And when his disciples James and John saw this, they said, 'Lord, wilt thou that we command fire to come down from heaven, and consume them, even as Elias did?' But he turned and rebuked them, and said, 'Ye know not what manner of spirit ye are of. For the Son of man is not come to destroy men's lives but to save them.' And they went to another village" (Luke 9:51–56).

The disciples believed, as do many today, that the God Jesus represented was the same as the God of the Old Testament. The God of Abraham, Isaac, and Jacob was a God who, according to their history, would permit you to destroy your enemies or anyone you have identified as an enemy of God. You could certainly do "as did Elias," and destroy anyone who offended God or any of his chosen people.

They were probably thinking something like this: "Who do these Samaritan dogs think they are dealing with here? Are they not going to offer us hospitality? Apparently they don't know who we are! Well, we will show them! Let's go talk to Jesus about the *fire from heaven* treatment. We'll show them who they're messing with and teach them a lesson they will never forget. We will call down fire from heaven and burn them, every man, women, and child. Yes, we will do a Sodom-and-Gomorrah number on them, so everybody will know they can't mess with us!"

Jesus reminded them that the God he represented was not a God of destruction but a God of love, tolerance, infinite patience, and forgiveness. Then he probably simply said, "Let's find another village." He also told the disciples that they had a spirit of prejudice, vengeance, judgment, hatred, and destruction in them—a spirit of "evil." The historic records would seem to suggest that the churches and many Christians are still operating under this same spirit. Instead of our wrath and judgment being directed at Samaritans, it is focused on anyone who disagrees with our theology and belief systems.

A recent event suggests that this "spirit of evil" still lurks at the heart of a segment of the Christian world. A very prominent and influential leader of what we call the "Christian Right" recently validated the truth of this observation. On national television, he essentially called upon the U.S. government to assassinate the president of a South American country because he disagreed with this elected leader's economic policy. If this religious leader had access to the power that Jesus had, the president of a foreign country would be dead. This Christian leader believes more in the God of the Old Testament than in God as Jesus defined him.

This segment of Christianity is currently involved in a bitter culture war with the larger American society, because they think they know God's will. We can safely conclude that if these Christians had full access to the power of creation that Jesus had, they would make everyone believe as they do, and behave the way they believe we ought to behave. They would not hesitate to use the power of the state to compel belief and punish deviance just as the early church did in the days of the Roman Empire in service to the God of Abraham, Isaac, and Jacob.

These contrasting images of God's fundamental nature (God of fear/God of love) are reinforced almost every Sunday in many churches. In one of the largest Pentecostal denominations, the practice is to have a general reading from the scripture after the invocation. The purpose of the reading is to create an atmosphere of hope and inspiration in the initial stages of the service. The established tradition is to read a passage from the book we have defined as the Psalms of David. Now David was a warrior-king, and his overall experience of God was that God was his secret weapon who made it possible for him to kill and conquer all of his enemies and the enemies of God's chosen people. Of course, Jesus's conceptualization of God is the exact opposite of David's version of God.

Jesus had to be aware of the disciples' tendency to misunderstand what he was trying to teach them. Therefore, to make sure that there was no misunderstanding about God's true nature, Jesus said, in the Gospel of John that if we knew him, then we should know and understand God. He said, quite clearly, "I and my Father are one" (John 10:30). His unambiguous statements about his relationship to God should have resolved this issue for all time in the minds of Christians. In addition, it should be obvious that Jesus tried to teach the disciples that God was the father of all people and that God's love for humanity was unconditional and unchanging. We are instructed to love unconditionally, to be accepting and tolerant of all things, and to be meek—not fighting even when you know you are right. He said that there was no justification for anger or violence toward anyone. Nonetheless, the disciples rejected Jesus's teaching, and we have chosen to follow their teachings and practices rather than Jesus's example.

Thus, the primary reason we do not have easy access to spiritual power (the power of God within to do miracles faithfully) is because we are spiritually immature. We are prone to judgment, quick to anger, and will even invoke the "wrath of God" on our children, spouses, and each other. Consequently our anger, judgments, and attitudes make it difficult if not impossible for us to access the power of the Holy Spirit within to "do the greater works." Because the founders of Christianity (Paul, the disciples, and their followers in time) missed Jesus's basic message about God's unconditional love and what this means in terms of our behavior toward each other, we have been misinformed.

Jesus is saying he has come to change our beliefs about God and his nature, and about who we are. He is saying that our perfect Father in heaven loves all of his children equally and that he wants us to manifest the love of God in our daily lives and in our interactions with each other. He expresses this sentiment quite clearly: "A new commandment I give unto you, That ye love one another; as I have loved you, that ye also love one another. By this shall all men know that ye are my disciples, if ye have love one to another" (John 13:34–35).

The disciples were confused because they were attempting to put "new wine in old bottles" (Mark 2:22). They were trying to understand God as Jesus was presenting the Father but still hold on to their traditional beliefs about God in the Judaic tradition. Their beliefs were formed in a culture based on the Mosaic Law. The idea of God, as the father of all humanity who loves all of his children equally, was a foreign concept to them.

John and James, who appeared to be among the more even-tempered of the disciples, wanted to destroy a village because the people disrespected them. This illustrates quite vividly that they truly did not understand Jesus's basic message.

Moreover, the time was short because this happened a week or so before the crucifixion. Jesus realized that if they had not gotten the message by that time, they would never get it. Jesus was upset and disappointed with them because of their unwillingness to give up their fixed ideas and beliefs which obviously stifled their abilities to do the greater work of miracles and healing as effectively as the seventy and the unnamed man.

The disciples continued to cling to the notion of God as Jesus presented him and the God of Abraham, Isaac, and Jacob as being one and the same. It was inconceivable to them that their fathers may have been wrong in their understanding of God and his true nature. The disciples steadfastly held on to their belief that God was a God of fear, death, and destruction rather than a God of love. These contradictory beliefs were thoroughly integrated into the basic theological foundation of the early church and have become structural elements of modern Christian theology and doctrine.

11

Fear of God and Modern Christianity

It is very difficult to have faith or confidence in the goodness and benevolence of someone or something that you fear. Jesus understood this. He tried to impress upon the minds of the disciples and Christians the idea of God as a loving father by continually referring to God as "your Father in heaven." In the famous "love your enemy" lesson (Matt. 5:44), he admonishes us to "be ye therefore perfect [in our love for all] even as your Father which is in heaven is perfect" (Matt. 5:48).

We see more dramatic evidence of how resistant the disciples were to Jesus's basic message that God is a perfect father who loves all of his children equally and that fear and unconditional love are mutually exclusive concepts. After Jesus's promises to the disciples that "ye shall receive power" were fulfilled, and the Holy Ghost was manifested on the day of Pentecost, Peter immediately began to preach the gospel. But Luke stated quite clearly that Peter and the disciples were not preaching a gospel based on Jesus's teaching: "And they continued steadfastly in the apostles' doctrine and fellowship, and in the breaking of bread, and in prayer. And fear came upon every soul: and many signs and wonders were done by the apostles" (Acts 2:42–43). Thus it is evident, according to scripture, that fear of God is an essential element in the Apostles' Doctrine.

It should be obvious that "the fear of God" is based on the belief that God will do horrible things to you if you do not obey the rules and that was not what Jesus taught. More importantly, there is nothing in Jesus's basic teaching or in the record of his life to suggest that the power of God is to be used to coerce, injure, intimidate, or kill any of his children for any reason whatsoever. Yet, in the earliest days of Christianity, this was the basic message from the disciples. The record clearly shows that they had the power to heal the sick and to do miracles. However, as Peter and the disciples developed a new religion based on the Apostles' Doctrine, they began to misuse the power God gave them. They used faith in

God, which they had inspired in people by their teaching and preaching and by the demonstrations of the power of the Holy Ghost, to control, punish, kill, and destroy those who violated their rules and doctrines.

We have a story in the Gospel of Mark concerning the death of a fig tree. Jesus approached the tree looking for fruit, which he knew would not be there, because figs were not in season. Jesus cursed the fig tree and by morning, it was dead. Peter noticed this and said "Master, behold, the fig tree which thou cursedst is withered away" (Mark 11:21). Although theologians have placed a certain interpretation on the meaning of this event that will be discussed later, Jesus explained to Peter and the disciples the realities of the power of belief (faith) coupled with thought and the manifestation of thoughts through the spoken word. He said that if any of us "shall not doubt in his heart, but believe that those things which he saith shall come to pass; he shall have whatever he saith" (Mark 11:23). The cursing of the fig tree was a story about faith and the power of the spoken word (thought made manifest). The lesson was not about using the power of God to kill and destroy. Jesus stated clearly that neither he nor God was interested in destroying the lives of any of God's children for any reason.

Jesus reinforced this message to his disciples and to us when Peter drew his sword and cut off the ear of the high priest's servant who was among those sent to bring Jesus for trial (John 18:10). In Matthew's gospel Jesus reminded the disciples and the modern Christian world that violence against any of your brothers or sisters for any reason was not in God's will or in Jesus's teaching. After Peter cut off the high priest's servant's ear, Jesus replaced the ear and said to Peter:

> "Put up again thy sword into his place: for all that take the sword shall perish with the sword. Thinkest thou that I cannot now pray to my Father, and he shall presently give me twelve legions of angels" (Matt.26:52–53).

Jesus was reminding the disciple about the integrity of his teaching—there are no valid reasons for fighting or killing another child of God. If warfare against an enemy was the issue, Jesus is saying that I could request that my father give me an invincible army (12 legions of angels or an army of 72, 000 immortal warriors one of whom destroyed an Assyrian army of 185,000 soldiers according to the Old Testament story 2 Kings 19:35).

It appears that Peter never learned the lessons of an unconditionally loving God, who abhors violence in his children. After he had been vested with the power of the Holy Ghost, he "spoke" the death of Ananias and Sapphira because they violated the rules the disciples had established concerning sharing in the

Christian community. Despite what Jesus had taught them about the sanctity of life, Peter failed to learn the lesson. History suggests that the Christian church did not learn this lesson either, and continues to miss the message even to this day.

Peter used the power of the Holy Ghost to harshly punish those early Christians who violated rules the disciples themselves had made. Not God's law but their rules! Jesus taught them something entirely different. So it is quite difficult to imagine that God, our perfect Father who loves us unconditionally, would kill us because we violated some rule that someone had identified as God's immutable law. If the penalty for sin or error in this world was instant death, then we all would be dead.

In the earliest days of Christianity, the disciples were the ultimate authority on Jesus and his teachings about God. The four Gospels had not been written at that time. Therefore the death of Ananias and Sapphira were perceived as ordained by God. They were killed by their belief in what the disciples taught them. They apparently held strong beliefs about God and what God required of them—beliefs generated in their minds by the disciple's teachings, healings, and other miracles. When Peter cursed them in the same way that Jesus cursed the fig tree, they both died. Jesus killed the fig tree to teach us about the awesome power of pure faith coupled with the spoken word. *The disciples abused this power for the sake of the rules they had established.* Jesus was never guilty of violating God's will as it relates to the sanctity of life and the true nature of eternal love. Peter and the disciples, however, were acting in accordance with the Old Testament law that disobedience under God's law was punishable by death.

Peter killed this couple out of his own hubris, arrogance, fear, and anger. He thought it proper that death be a suitable punishment for disobeying religious authority because this is what he had been taught under the law. Moses reported to the people that the God of Abraham, Isaac, and Jacob made the following promises to the children of Israel concerning disobedience: "But it shall come to pass, if thou wilt not hearken unto the voice of the Lord thy God, to observe to do all his commandments and his statures which I command thee this day; that all these curses shall come upon thee, and overtake thee" (Deut. 28:15). Following this statement, Moses laid out fifty-two verses of detailed curses that God promised would afflict the children of Israel, including a return into bondage to the Egyptians as punishment for disobedience.

The record suggests that the children of Israel were unfaithful and disobedient at every turn, but the vast majority of the curses promised by Moses were unfulfilled. Nevertheless, it should be obvious that the disciples' fear-based doctrine was not based on Jesus's teaching or his example but on their beliefs and commitment to the Mosaic Law. According to Jesus, God forgives transgressions in this life (Matt. 6:14–15). He does not kill you if you are disobedient. An essential question for Christians, then, is whose version of God is true?

12

The Power of Fear and Unbelief

It is essential that Christians who aspire to be reliable healers in the manner of Jesus address this issue relating to the confusion in Christian theology about God's true nature. As a human father with three daughters, I have consistently tried to show them unconditional love, patience, tolerance, gentleness, understanding, and trustworthiness. Because they know this is my character, they have faith, trust, and confidence in me. I have often said to them that if they took my best characteristics as a parent and multiply them by a factor of perfection, they would have some vague sense of God's relationship with them and a good sense of how he regards them.

On the other hand, if I had killed or tortured some of my children because of disobedience or mistakes they made, no matter what the justification may have been, my daughters would fear me but could never fully trust me. If the capacity for great anger, violence, harsh judgment, and mass destruction were aspects of my character, they would fear me. However, it would be very difficult or impossible for them to have faith in me or to have confidence in my love for them. There is a graphic demonstration of the awesome power of doubt and unbelief to neutralize the willingness and power of God to work on our behalf:

> "And it came to pass, that when Jesus had finished these parables, he departed thence. And when he was come into his own country, he taught them in their synagogue, insomuch that they were astonished, and said 'Whence hath this man this wisdom, and these mighty works? Is not this the carpenter's son? Is not his mother called Mary? And his brethren, James, and Joses, and Simon, and Judas? And his sisters, are they not all with us? Whence then hath this man all these things?' And they were offended in him. But Jesus said unto them, 'A prophet is not without honour, save in his own country, and in his own house.' And he did not many mighty works there because of their unbelief" (Matt. 13:53–58).

This passage of scripture provides us with an excellent illustration of the power of confusion about the true nature of God (Jesus), and its ability to undermine faith/belief and to create unbelief. If we do not believe who Jesus is and the truth of what he is teaching us about himself and God, there is sufficient doubt to neutralize the power of God within us to do miracles. If we have doubts about the worthiness of the individual in need of healing, we will not be able to help their unbelief. The woman defining herself as an atheist who received a miracle of healing of her kidney is a powerful validation of the truth I have attempted to convey about the importance of the healer's absolute faith in God, the perfect Father, and his unconditional love and faithfulness to all of his children—as Jesus has taught us.

Jesus had major concerns about the disciple's lack of faith and confidence in him and his teachings. At the beginning of his ministry, Jesus declared that "the time is fulfilled, and the kingdom of God is at hand: repent ye, and believe the gospel" (Mark 1:15). He was saying to the world that he was the fulfillment of the prophecy. But the second piece of important information was that the kingdom of God, in the person of Jesus, had come into the physical world. And along with the knowledge found in the kingdom, an aspect of God in the form of Jesus was manifested. Jesus also said to the world, "Repent ye and believe the gospel," and Mark reports that he immediately called the disciples as his primary students and assistants.

They were Jesus's closest companions who shared with him the last three years of his earthly journey. They shared his experiences and witnessed the miracles of healing and his other great works. They received intensive training and instruction from Jesus about many things. Jesus gave them new and different information about God and his true nature. He introduced them to the concept of divine power and how this power is to be used in the service of all of God's children. He taught them about God's love and how this love is expressed in the world. He also taught them the meaning of true worship. Jesus also informed them that he was an aspect of God made manifest in the physical world, thus identifying himself as God incarnate.

Above all else, Jesus tried to teach them about his purpose in coming into the world. Nevertheless, there is strong evidence that the disciples had a difficult time with repentance or giving up their old ideas and beliefs about God. They did not believe in Jesus's divinity or that he was God manifested among them as he defined himself when he said "I and my Father are one" (John 10:30). According to the records, their unbelief would manifest at every opportunity. Again we are going to the stories about the two miracles of fishes and loaves because they are classic examples of the disciples' denial and unbelief.

There is the report in the Gospel of Matthew that a great multitude of people had gathered to be healed and hear Jesus speak. According to scripture, "Jesus went forth, and saw a great multitude, and was moved with compassion toward them, and he healed their sick." When the evening came, the disciples informed him that they were going to send the people away to find food. Jesus responded, "They need not depart: give ye them to eat." So the disciples brought Jesus a boy's lunch—five rolls and two fish. Jesus told the disciples to sit the people down in an orderly fashion. He blessed the food and fed five thousand people (Matt. 14:14–21).

About two weeks later, they were involved in a similar situation. Jesus remarked that this great multitude had been with them for three days and had nothing to eat. He expressed clearly to the disciples that he would not send them away hungry. "And his disciples said unto him, 'Whence should we have so much bread in the wilderness, as to fill so great a multitude'" (Matt. 15:33). This is truly a remarkable response from the disciples. Jesus expressed a clear intent that he would not send the multitude away without feeding them. Nevertheless, they wondered how Jesus was going to feed them!

The question in my mind is how was it possible for them to so readily forget who Jesus was and what he was capable of doing? Peter, the take-charge guy, did order John and James to go find a lunch and bring it to Jesus while the people were being organized. But they had doubts about Jesus and continued to manifest unbelief. They repressed all memory of the previous miracle and denied in their hearts and mind any experience that was too difficult for them to comprehend. They simply forgot that Jesus was God incarnate and nothing was impossible for him!

Thus, the story continues. After the first miracle of fish and loaves, we have the report of Jesus making his way across the lake without a boat. As he came near the disciples' boat, they saw him walking across the water; they believed they were seeing a ghost. Their immediate response was fear and doubt. They would rather believe in ghosts than to acknowledge that Jesus was truly who he said he was: God incarnate. There are scriptural evidences that this pattern continued throughout Jesus's ministry.

Finally, we come to the crucifixion and the resurrection. Again we see the drama of the disciples' doubt and unbelief being played out. Mark reports that after the crucifixion, the women went to the sepulcher to anoint Jesus's body with oil. When they got to the tomb, they found that the stone had been rolled away from the entrance to the tomb. They had an encounter with an angel who gave them specific instructions: "But go your way, tell his disciples and Peter that he goeth before you into Galilee: there shall ye see him, as he said unto you" (Mark 16:7). True to form, the disciples responded in typical fashion: "And they, when they heard that he was alive, and had been seen of her, believed not" (Mark 16:11). It seems remarkable to me that the disciples were so adamant and steadfast in their doubts and unbelief. The report continues: "Afterward he appeared unto the eleven as they sat at meat, and upbraided them with their unbelief and hardness of heart, because they believed not them which had seen him after he was risen" (Mark 16:14).

I am suggesting that the disciples continued to miss the message that Jesus brought them through his ministry of teaching, miracles, and healing. It was difficult for them to believe that all of their cherished convictions about God and humanity were essentially wrong. The information they rejected was related to the conflict concerning the questions of Jesus's true identity. The issue is captured very well in the following passage from John:

> "Then the Jews took up stones again to stone him. Jesus answered them, 'Many good works have I shewed you from my Father; for which of those works do ye stone me?' The Jews answered him, saying, 'For a good work we stone ye not; but for blasphemy; and because thou, being a man, makest thyself God.' Jesus answered them, 'Is it not written in your law, "I said, Ye are gods?" If he called them gods, unto whom the word of God came, and the scripture cannot be broken; Say ye of him, whom the Father hath sanctified, and sent into the world, Thou blasphemest; because I said, I am the Son of God? If I do not the works of my Father, believe me not. But if I do, though ye believe not me, believe the works: that ye may know, and believe that the Father is in me, and I in him' (John 10:31–38).

According to John's report, the people did not repent (change their thinking and beliefs) and could not believe. They continued to question Jesus's divinity. The record suggests that the disciples did not change their beliefs either. Again, I remind you that the scripture clearly states that "God created man in his own image, in the image of God created him; male and female created he them" (Gen. 1:27). Nonetheless, in the Apostles' Doctrine according to Acts, the divinity of humanity is also denied. Thus it becomes difficult or impossible to truly believe that we have the power to consistently do the greater works of miracles and healing as Jesus instructed us.

The disciples, like most of us, were firmly grounded in the natural world and in their cultural and religious ideology. As a result, they were unable to transcend (repent) their own cultural and religious belief systems. They observed all of the things Jesus did but could not overcome their doubts and unbelief. They experienced the awe and wonder of Jesus miracles, but could not believe either for his sake or for "the very works' sake." It should be apparent that this element of doubt or unbelief has distorted Jesus's fundamental message to the extent that judging the world—exacting harsh punishment of people who have been judged evil or guilty of something—has become common practice in the Christian world. Moreover, we are unwilling to forsake judgment and to love unconditionally. As a result, our false beliefs and attitudes become major obstacles to our ability to do miracles of healing as a routine aspect of our Christian ministries. It is apparent that the apostles' lack of comprehension of Jesus's gospel is the basic source of the confusion about the nature of God and our purpose in being.

After the manifestation of the Holy Ghost, Peter went out and preached his first great sermon. A casual examination of the content of his sermon makes it obvious how completely he missed the message. In this sermon, Peter defined Jesus, who was the creative aspect of God manifested in the world (the Word made flesh), as merely "a man approved of God" (Acts 2:22). Therefore, it is crystal clear that Peter's fundamental unbelief concerning the divine nature of Jesus and all of humanity has become a key structural fallacy in the Apostles' Doctrine. And this fundamental fallacy has been structured into the basic fabric of mainstream Christian theology.

13

The Apostles' Doctrine

If we are to understand how the power to do reliable and consistent miracles of healing was lost, we must take a closer look at the phenomenon described by Luke as the "Apostles' Doctrine." The Acts of the Apostles was Luke's report on the early history of the church and an account of the apostles' role in the spread of the gospel. At the beginning of Acts, Luke records an additional conversation between Jesus and the disciples:

> "To whom also he shewed himself alive after his passion by many infallible proofs, being seen of them forty days, and speaking of the things pertaining to the kingdom of God. And, being assembled together with them, commanded them that they should not depart from Jerusalem but wait for the promise of the Father, which, saith he, 'Ye have heard of me. For John truly baptized with water; but ye shall be baptized with the Holy Ghost not many days hence…And," saith he, 'it is not for you to know the times or the season, which the Father hath put in his own power. But ye shall receive power, after that the Holy Ghost is come upon you: and ye shall be my witnesses unto me both in Jerusalem, and in all Judea, and in Samaria, and unto the uttermost part of the earth'" (Acts 1:3–5, 7–8).

God's plan was for Jesus to come and teach us the truth about God and the kingdom of heaven by words and deeds. Through Jesus's ministry, God taught the disciples and the world about divine love, patience, tolerance, and forgiveness. Jesus defined the attributes of God through his actions and behavior in the world, and taught us about our status as children of God, and about our entitlements.

It is essential that we understand the significance of Jesus's continual characterization of God as a perfect father. Jesus defines God in these terms so that we can better understand his true relationship to us. As previously stated, human parents have obligations and responsibilities to their children that are not in any way dependent upon the children's behavior. Jesus clearly states that we can depend on God to faithfully fulfill his parental responsibilities and obligations to all of his children because he has given us the following instructions and assurances:

> "Ask, and it shall be given you; seek, and ye shall find; knock, and it shall be opened unto you: For every one that asketh receiveth; and he that seeketh findeth; and to him that knocketh it shall be opened. Or what man is there of you, whom if his son ask bread, will he give him a stone? Or if he ask a fish, will he give him a serpent? If ye then, being evil, know how to give good gifts unto your children, how much more shall your Father which is in heaven give good things to them that ask him?" (Matt. 7:7–11).

Jesus also reminds us of our responsibilities to one another: to love one another as he has loved us. Jesus told the disciples that after they received power and the Holy Ghost, they were to be his witnesses to the world. A witness is one who has seen or heard something and can give reliable evidence of the truth of what was seen or heard. However, there is ample evidence that the disciples were not reliable witnesses because of their persistent unbelief and because they did not give up their old beliefs and learn what Jesus was trying to teach them. As a result, they could not teach us what they did not know or believe.

Matthew reports that they saw him after the resurrection, but some of the disciples continued to doubt (Matt. 28:17). Mark stated, "Afterward he appeared unto the eleven as they sat at meat, and upbraided them with their unbelief and hardness of heart" (Mark 16:14). Jesus rebuked the disciples again about their doubts and unwillingness to change their ways of thinking. Throughout Jesus's ministry, they were adamant about maintaining their false belief systems, no matter what Jesus taught or demonstrated to them concerning his divinity. Luke's report indicates that after the resurrection, the disciples' doubt and unbelief remained essentially unchanged.

When the women told the disciples that Jesus had indeed risen, they did not believe them. And when Jesus appeared in their midst and said, "Peace be unto you," their reaction was identical to the reaction of Jesus walking on water. Instead of rejoicing, Luke observed that "They were terrified and affrighted, and they supposed they had seen a spirit" (Luke 24:37). The disciples refused to believe that Jesus was true to his word and rose from the dead. Resurrection would be a simple feat for God but impossible for a human being. It is easy to see that their faithlessness and unbelief were directly related to their doubts about Jesus's divinity. If Jesus was indeed the divine Son of God, he was immortal and could not die. It is a very sad commentary, but they were much more comfortable with the notion that they saw a ghost rather than believe what Jesus taught them about who and what he was.

After the "fall" of the Holy Ghost (Acts 2:1–4), Peter went out and preached his first sermon. It was a powerful sermon, with many references to the prophesies of Joel, David, and the Old Testament. Luke provides the following commentary on Peter's sermon: "And with many other words did he testify and exhort, saying, 'Save yourselves from this untoward generation.' Then they that gladly received his words were baptized: and the same day there was added unto them about three thousand souls. And they continued stedfastly in the Apostles' Doctrine and fellowship, and in breaking of bread and in prayer. And fear came upon every soul: and many signs and wonders were done by the apostles" (Acts 2:40–43).

Luke was aware from the very beginning that Peter and the other disciples had strayed from Jesus's gospel almost immediately. Jesus stated that there were only three commandments he believed were essential for us to master: to love God with all of our heart, soul, and mind; to love our neighbor as ourselves; and to love one another as he had loved us (Matt. 22:37–39, John 15:12). The first deviation Peter made from the gospel of Jesus Christ was his identification of Jesus as "a man approved of God among you" (Acts 2:22). Jesus's divinity is compromised under this doctrine. Then Peter asserted that "Therefore let all the house of Israel know assuredly, that God hath made this same Jesus, whom you crucified, both Lord and Christ" (Acts 2:36).

Implicit in Peter's statement was that God will surely make the entire house of Israel pay dearly for this grievous offense. Moreover, he reinforced the notion of fear by quoting extensively from the prophet Joel, whose prophecies, according to scripture, were time- and place-specific and not related to Jesus or his ministry. Consequently, fear was introduced into the Apostles' Doctrine. Then in his second major sermon, Peter immediately reconnected people to the God of Abraham, Isaac, and Jacob (Acts 3:13); the God of their fathers with whom they (the disciples) were most familiar and comfortable. Peter and the other disciples then made some additional regulations to supplement the religious rules with which they were already familiar under the law.

They isolated themselves into a separate community, and prayed and fellowshipped with each other daily. Among the rules they established was one regarding contributing wealth and property to the church, supposedly for the common good. Although Jesus had said that every child of God could rely on the Father in heaven to provide for our needs, the disciples initiated the tradition of reliance on other men and a man-made institution (the church), which has resulted in wars, killings, corruption, sexual abuse, and divisions among God's children. More importantly, the disciples began to use the power of God to do terrible things to people who did not obey the rules. Luke described the rules of community ownership of wealth and property in the following manner:

> "And the multitude of them that believed were of one heart and of one soul: neither said any of them that aught of the things which he possessed was his own; but they had all things common. And with great power gave the apostles witness of the resurrection of the Lord Jesus: with great grace upon them all. Neither was there any among them that lacked: for as many as were possessors of lands, or houses sold them, and brought the prices of the things that were sold, and laid them down at the apostles' feet: and distribution was made unto every man according to need" (Acts 4:32–35).

The idea of a Christian community developing regulations regarding the responsibilities of the group for the material and spiritual well-being of the members of the group may be a good idea. However, it was not God's rule. Jesus understood the modern maxim concerning the corruptive nature of power. And as I have previously stated, the truth of this principle was vividly demonstrated in the death of Ananias and Sapphira for failure to abide by the new rules contained in the Apostles' Doctrine. It is important for us to remember Jesus said quite plainly that "the Son of man is not come to destroy men's lives, but to save them" (Luke 9:56).

Peter and the disciples used the power of the Holy Ghost and the witness of Jesus Christ, along with fear and guilt, to compel the people of their day to accept the apostles' doctrine or belief system. Implied in the message was that if you do not repent and believe the apostles' version of the message, God will do horrible things to you. In another powerful sermon, following the healing of the man who was born lame (Acts 3:1), Peter completely nullified Jesus's definition of God as a perfect father who loves his children unconditionally when he attributed the miracle to the God of the Old Testament, who was the God they believed in, rather than to God as Jesus defined him:

> "And as the lame man which was healed held Peter and John, all the people ran together unto them in the porch that is called Solomon's, greatly wondering. And when Peter saw it, he answered unto the people, 'Ye men of Israel, why marvel ye at this? Or why look ye so earnestly on us, as though by our own power or holiness we had made this man to walk? The God of Abraham, and of Isaac, and of Jacob, the God of our fathers, hath glorified his Son Jesus; whom ye delivered up, and denied him in the presence of Pilate, when he was

determined to let him go. But ye denied the Holy One and the Just, and desired a murderer to be granted unto you; and killed the Prince of life, whom God has raised from the dead; whereof we are witnesses'" (Acts 3:11–15).

All of the sermons Peter preached were liberally "laced" with his anger, guilt, and fear, and had the effect of creating guilt and fear of God in the minds and hearts of all who heard them. There was also an element of the self-righteous arrogance so common in the history of religious groups: we and only we know the way. It is obvious that this was a totally different message from that which Jesus gave us through his humble and loving behavior toward us and through his teachings about himself and God. Misinformation about God's true character and nature was mixed in the Apostles' Doctrine.

The messages contained in Peter's sermons were a direct contradiction of what Jesus had taught the disciples and the people of his day about God and his purposes for humanity. The disciples could not receive Jesus's basic message because the theology of the law and Old Testament traditions were a firmly established aspect of their belief systems. The images of God as a God of fear and retribution were essential elements in the religious history of the Jews. Jesus never used the power vested in him by God to hurt or destroy people. Peter, who history recognizes as the father of the Church, used the power of the Holy Ghost to kill, coerce, intimidate, and destroy, thus setting a precedent that other church leaders followed. Subsequently, according to history, the Holy Ghost eventually withdrew from the church and from the world shortly after the establishment of the early church and did not return until 1906 during the Azusa Street Revival.

The record also suggests that the apostles shifted to the notion of repentance to a change motivated by guilt for past sins as opposed to Jesus's definition of repentance as a change of mind from learning new information and observing his powerful demonstrations of God's love and power. Miracles of healing were key elements of the charge Jesus gave to the disciples and the modern church after the resurrection. The record will show that it was Jesus's intention that the healing tradition should continue. Let me quote the last words Jesus gave the disciples, according to the four Gospels. Matthew makes the following report:

> "Then the eleven disciples went away into Galilee, into a mountain where Jesus had appointed them. And when they saw him, they worshipped him but some doubted. And Jesus came and spake unto them, saying, "All power is given unto me in heaven and in earth. Go ye therefore, and teach all nations, baptizing them in the name of the Father, the Son, and the Holy Ghost.

Teaching them to observe all things I have commanded you: and lo, I am with you always, even unto the end of the world" (Matt. 28:16–20).

Then according to Mark's Gospel, Jesus said:

> "Go ye into all the world, and preach the gospel to every creature. He that believeth and is baptized shall be saved: But he that believeth not shall be damned. And these signs shall follow them that believe; In my name shall they cast out devils: they shall speak with new tongues; They shall take up serpents; and if they drink any deadly thing, it shall not hurt them; they shall lay hands on the sick and they shall recover" (Mark 16:15–18).

John, who seemed to be the only one of the disciples who was fully convinced of Jesus's divinity and thus demonstrated that he understood the message better than his brethren, comments after the resurrection: "And many signs truly did Jesus in the presence of his disciples, which are not written in this book. But these are written, that ye might believe that Jesus is the Christ, the Son of God: and that believing ye might have life through his name" (John 20:30–31). I believe that the lack of faithfulness to Jesus's teaching has hindered our abilities to do the greater works. Instead of following the guidance of Jesus, who lovingly informed us that "I am the way the truth and the life" (John 14:6), we have chosen to follow the other teachers from the Bible and the theologians who have followed the Apostles' Doctrine.

14

Jesus: The Only Authority on God

Jesus paints a picture of God as our perfect Father. Based on Jesus's teaching and his behavior in the world, God is kind, gentle, loving, and forgiving. He is a father who is patient and tolerant enough to give his children all the time they need to learn what they need to know. In the Gospel of John, Jesus was even more direct in his attempts to resolve the lingering confusion about God's true nature and to give us a very clear and unambiguous picture of exactly who or what God is, and his true nature:

> "Philip said unto him, 'Lord, shew us the Father, and it sufficeth us.' Jesus saith unto him, 'Have I been so long time with you and yet hast thou not known me, Philip? He that hath seen me hath seen the Father; and how sayest thou then, Shew us the Father?'" (John 14:8–9).

Although Jesus had told the disciples earlier in John 10:30, "I and my Father are one," neither the disciples nor modern-day saints take Jesus's words literally. We are much more comfortable with God created in our own image and likeness, rather than God as Jesus has defined him. But Jesus was quite clear when he said, "I and my Father are one." What this means is that they are not different but are one and the same. God's nature and temperament has to be the same as Jesus's nature and temperament. Nevertheless, these contradictory beliefs about Jesus and about God's true nature became a part of our current religious ideologies through the Apostles' Doctrine. Furthermore, as this doctrine was integrated into the structure of the early church, the power God gave to the disciples was not used in a loving and nurturing way. It was used by the early church leaders to control and intimidate, kill and destroy. At the center of this gospel as it was initially preached by Peter was the God of Abraham, Isaac, and Jacob. Thus, the reality of God, as Jesus defined him through his teachings and his behavior, has been obscured by these contradictory versions of God.

Many Christians believe that to question the validity of any portion of the Bible is blasphemy. Nevertheless, contradictory concepts and definitions with totally different meanings cannot both be true. Let me give one example of the human tendency for eyewitness reports of the same event to differ so much you are forced to question the reliability of the reports. Both Luke and Matthew were present when Jesus made an observation that "the harvest is truly plenteous but the labourers are few" (Matt. 9:37; Luke 10:2).

Matthew reports that Jesus sent the twelve disciples on the healing mission while Luke reported that he sent an "unnamed seventy." If the reports are of the same event, both cannot be true. We assume that all of the disciples knew how to count, because you cannot mistake twelve of anything for seventy. We have to question the motives of the disciples or their followers in reporting dramatically different versions of the same event because radically different reports of the same event cannot both be true. But Christians have trained themselves not to question the validity or truth of any of these reports. We can safely assume that Luke's version is true because the disciples were unable to cast out demons, according to the records, while the seventy reported success in healing these conditions.

There is ample evidence that there are major distortions in the reports about Jesus's life and purpose in the four Gospels. There is also evidence that the disciples had a great deal of difficulty understanding who Jesus was and what he was trying to teach them. Jesus told them that he and God were one. They believed that God, the creator, could do anything. Nevertheless, when Jesus created enough food to feed a great multitude of people from a single lunch, they were astounded. As previously discussed, their unbelief was conclusively demonstrated a few weeks later in a similar situation when they ask Jesus where they are going to get bread in the wilderness to feed all the people:

> "Then Jesus called his disciples unto him and said, 'I have compassion on the multitude, because they continued now with me for three days, and have nothing to eat: and I will not send them away fasting, lest they faint in the way.' And his disciples say unto him, Whence should we have so much bread in the wildness to fill so great a multitude?" (Matt.15:32–33).

The disciples' remarkable response to Jesus's declared intent to feed this multitude of people demonstrates a degree of denial that is difficult to understand. It suggests that even in the presence of Jesus, they doubted everything he said and suppressed all memory of anything Jesus did that caused too much conflict with their version of reality or their deeply held beliefs. They also failed to understand what Jesus was trying to teach them about God and the kingdom of God. It would appear that they did not grasp any of the basic information and knowledge Jesus tried to give them. If they were not convinced that Jesus could duplicate any miracle he performed as often as was necessary, it is safe to say that they missed the message entirely.

Thus, the concept of God as a perfect father with unending love and compassion for all of his children in every circumstance was incomprehensible to the disciples who believed so strongly in the God of Abraham, Isaac, and Jacob. They could not understand a God of love as Jesus manifested him. There is nothing fearful about absolute unconditional love. If God's character is fixed and unchanging, he would always demonstrate love and compassion for them in all circumstances. Conversely, God would not do cruel and horrible things to any of his children at any time under any circumstance.

Jesus's teachings were a reflection of his own character. He was teaching us to be like him and thus be like God. If we truly understood the Sermon on the Mount, we would gain a tremendous amount of insight about what Jesus meant when he said, "I am the way, the truth and the life: no man cometh unto the Father, but by me" (John 14:6). The theologians will say that many of the words of Jesus contained in the four Gospels speak of the same God found in the Old Testament. The God of Abraham, Isaac, and Jacob will certainly cast you into hell where you will suffer eternal torment if you do not repent of your sins and follow the rules as they defined them. However, it would appear that Jesus is giving us an entirely different conceptualization of God.

Although we have many references in the Old Testament that suggest that God does change his mind about many things, this would suggest uncertainty in God's mind and character. Men are ignorant and uncertain about many things, but God is unlike man! There is common theological agreement that God is eternal, omnipotent, omnipresent, and omniscient. Eternal means that God's character is fixed and unchanging; like Jesus, God is the same today, yesterday, and forever. Thus, an unconditionally loving father possessing these attributes knows the consequences of all things and could never make a mistake requiring repentance. He could never be a God of death and destruction and a God of unconditional love!

There is one thing all biblical scholars and theologians should know. They should know the history of the Bible and the history of the church. They know that the four Gospels were written from fifty to ninety years after the death and resurrection of Jesus. It is also a fact that everyone who had control of the Bible has edited it in support of their own theology.

Entire gospels were eliminated and others included based on a particular doctrinal or theological purpose. Very few ordinary Christians are aware that Thomas wrote a Gospel or that many of the early Christian communities had their own individual New Testament books that were different from each other. For example, few of you have ever heard of the Apocalypse of Peter or the Epistle of Barnabas. Nor do non-Catholics know anything bout the Shepherd of Hermas or the Didache. The Roman Catholic Bible has additions to Esther as well as books of Baruch, Tobit, Sirach, Judith, Wisdom, and Maccabees that you will not find in the Protestant Bibles. Moreover, the Catholic version is the absolutely true and only word of God. And so is the Protestant's version! It is all a matter of belief for them, the truth is unimportant. But Jesus said that there is a truth and that we should know it.

In the early Church history, there were constant conflicts about what constituted the real and true word of God. After the Roman emperor Constantine was converted to Christianity by his wife, he became the secular head of the Church. In the year AD 325 he called all of the warring factions among the Church leaders to the Council of Nicaea to try and resolve the doctrinal conflicts in the early church. This group of men decided what the authentic "word of God" was and what was appropriate for inclusion in the Christian canon. They also decided what among the various scriptures relied upon by the various factions, were to be considered as the inerrant word of God and what was to be considered as heresy. God did not make this decision; men did!

The Council of Nicaea also developed the Nicene Creed, which is a summary of basic Christian beliefs. This creed, developed by men, has become the statement of faith and commitment by which men profess repentance. It is part of the ritual of salvation administered to "sinners" in many Christian denominations. It is possible that God inspired the Nicene Creed but Jesus had nothing to say about it! The emperor Constantine did what every "power" that had exclusive control of the Bible has done. His influence was used to shape and change the report so that it fit the prevailing belief system.

Historically, this pattern has continued. Any notion that did not fit the ideological beliefs or the cultural practices of the times were deleted or changed. Moreover, for a long time, the church restricted access to the Bible to a few trusted clergy upon the penalty of death. The scholar who first translated the Bible from Latin, the language of the priesthood, to German, the language of the common people, was excommunicated, tortured, and killed by the church he served—Christians who, by definition, were followers of Christ. Any objective analysis will reveal quite clearly that the justification for this type of behavior has its genesis in the theology of the Old Testament. Thus, it is evil related to structure rather than a failing of the Christians of that era. They were simply acting on policies which evolved out of their theology. It would be a very far stretch of logic to believe that Jesus would ever condone an act of this nature on one of God's beloved children for any reason. But according to the biblical record, the God of Abraham, Isaac, and Jacob would!

Theologians and biblical scholars also know that the written Gospels were based on oral accounts that were second- or third-hand reports. Before the time of Moses, there were no written records of anything. Human beings did not know how to write. The histories were passed on to future generations through a process known as oral tradition. In effect, they told stories about themselves and many believed the stories to be true. The reality is that all of our stories are subjective in nature, including what we have agreed is true. At times, we choose to believe our stories are true because they constitute our history! However, even though we all may agree on a particular truth, our unanimous agreement does not make it true.

Just because the stories people told each other were believed to be true, it does not follow that they were true. It was established scientific fact at that time that the world was flat and the sun revolved around the earth. Everyone believed this, but it was never true. Thus it is certain that none of the scribes, prophets, or patriarchs in the Old Testament who told their stories about God knew more about God than Jesus. Jesus makes this point quite clear when he said that they could not know God, because unlike him (Jesus), they had never seen God: "Not that any man hath seen the Father, save he which is of God, he hath seen the Father" (John 6:46).

It would seem logical that if the disciples misunderstood the basic lessons about God and his nature while Jesus was with them, they were certain to have major distortions in their memories of the message fifty to ninety years later. By the time the four gospels were written, the Apostles' Doctrine had been thoroughly integrated into the doctrine and theology of the early church. God, who is the central focus of worship, had taken on more of the character of the God of the Old Testament than God as Jesus revealed Him. It would also appear that some of the key elements of the Apostles' Doctrine had been interjected into some of the written records of Jesus's teachings.

In doing the works that God sent him to do, Jesus was in constant conflict with the prevailing religious practices and traditions. He healed on the Sabbath and interacted with lepers, Samaritans, and others who were defined by the law as unclean. In the Sermon on the Mount, he taught what God required of us; things which were in direct contradiction to the law as it was understood at that time. He framed his teaching in a direct way so that we could not miss its implications. Jesus said, "Ye have heard that it hath been said by them of old times" and then added, "but I say unto you…" He would then teach us something that was the opposite of what was taught by "them of old times." I believe that he was speaking about what the Pharisees, Sadducees, and scribes had been taught under the Mosaic Law.

Biblical scholars and Christians believe the Law was given to Moses by God and that every word of it is the word of God and therefore true. Nonetheless, Jesus is saying in the Sermon on the Mount that Moses obviously misunderstood what God "told" him, because he told us something entirely different from what Moses and the scribes have said were God's immutable laws. After all, Jesus said, "I am giving you the true word from God." John validates this resolution of this conflict when he said, "The law was given by Moses, but grace and truth came by Jesus Christ. No man hath seen God at any time, the only begotten Son, which is in the bosom of the Father, he hath declared him" (John 1:17–18). However, most of our Christian doctrines are based on the very laws Jesus clearly repudiated during the Sermon on the Mount.

The fifth chapter of John says that Jesus said he is the only authority on any issues related to God. After Jesus healed the man who had been lame for thirty-eight years, the Jews questioned his authority to do things the way he was doing them. In a long discourse, Jesus asserted his authority to heal on the Sabbath. He reinforced the basic truth that God was his father, and that they were one. Moreover, Jesus makes the point that none of the Jews knew anything about God because "Ye have neither heard his voice at any time, nor seen his shape" (John 5:37). Jesus continues this theological conflict with the religious authorities in the sixth chapter of John when he said, "It is written in the prophets, 'And they shall be all taught of God.' Every man therefore that hath heard, and learned of the Father, cometh unto me. Not that any man hath seen the Father, save he which is of God, he hath seen the Father" (John 6:45–46).

Jesus again states that no man has seen God except him, including all of the patriarchs, prophets, and the apostles. Notwithstanding the fact that they apparently got it all wrong. Jesus said, "'This is the bread which cometh down from heaven, that a man may eat thereof, and not die. I am the living bread which came down from heaven: if any man eat of this bread, he shall live for ever: and the bread that I will give is my flesh, which I will give for the life of the world'" (John 6:50–51).

We must remember Jesus was the Word made flesh. When Jesus speaks of his flesh, he is speaking about his words. A word is a thought made manifest in the physical world in the form of sound. Jesus, then, is the creative power of God, manifested in the form of flesh. His words are God's words. In Jesus's words there is power to do all things. He is saying that we must consume his flesh (words), and digest them (make them be an integrated aspect of our very being, our thoughts and purpose). The power to heal the sick and cast out demons is inherent in understanding Jesus's words. There is also the power to do miracles.

God's creative, miraculous power is not in theology or doctrine. Theology is the academic study of what we believe we know about God from the perspective of a particular religion. However, I believe that the only true theology for a Christian is one based on Jesus's works and words. Doctrine is what we teach about God and his rules of behavior for us, and the rule of worship. In reality it is only what we think we know about God's regulations. Jesus said that true worship is of the Spirit; it is not in ritual, structure, or forms.

Although we may tell ourselves that all Christian theology and doctrine is a derivative of God's word, the reality is that they were created by the minds of men. The rituals of salvation known as "the Sinner's Prayer" or the Nicene Creed was developed by a group of theologians. It is doctrine created by man, but we teach it as if it is the authoritative and true word of God. I am suggesting that the only true doctrine is one based on what Jesus taught us.

The basic theology of modern Christianity was founded on the Apostles' Doctrine, not on the gospel of Jesus Christ. As a result, the harsh, judgmental, and fearful God of the Old Testament is a central element in this doctrine and has been thoroughly integrated into the fabric and structure of the modern church. From its inception, the early church was established on a doctrine of fear rather than unconditional love. An examination of church history suggests that this structural flaw in the foundation remains today. Therefore, the fundamental power of the Holy Ghost is not available to us in a reliable fashion because we are still confused about God's nature. Moreover, we have not learned to love one another as Jesus has loved us. I believe that the modern-day church does not truly understand the knowledge of good and evil from Jesus's perspective. The church has lost the power to do consistent miracles of healing because of unbelief related to Jesus and his teaching.

For example, the leaders of the early church believed that Christianity was the true and God-ordained way to salvation. They also believed that their mission from God was to convert the world to the true path. Shortly after Christianity became the official religion of Rome, the Catholic Church used the full power of the State to torture and kill anyone they deemed nonbelievers, heretics, and enemies of the faith. This was behavior in the true spirit of the Apostles' Doctrine—the spirit and tradition of the Old Testament—but it is alien to the Spirit of Jesus Christ.

Jesus used his relationship with the Samaritans, one of the original tribes of Israel, to teach a totally different lesson concerning our beliefs about the true way to salvation. The Jews believed that Samaritans were heretics and therefore unclean. They believed this because the Samaritans worshipped God differently than the Jews. They also followed a different set of beliefs in their rituals and ceremonies. But Jesus had a loving and very personal relationship with them. We know that Jesus held them in high regard because he used the Samaritans to teach some of God's most important lessons.

They were used to teach the lessons of God's true nature (Spirit); the nature of true worship (spirit and truth); the nature of true love and brotherhood (the Good Samaritan); and God's love and compassion for all of his children (Jesus's refusal to permit the disciples to destroy the Samaritan village). I believe we have missed entirely the fundamental lessons in Jesus's relationship with Samaritans. The basic message to the children of Israel was that the Samaritans, who are defined as unclean heretics who will certainly die and go to hell, are the children God loves as much as he loves you. Unconditional love for all of God's children is the first condition that must be met by Christians committed to doing the greater works of healing; giving up judgment is the second. The third is the willingness to forgive all, in case you have judged. And the fourth is to have faith in God, your perfect father as Jesus has defined him.

It should be obvious to every teacher and preacher of Christian theology and doctrine that this issue is at the heart of the confusion about God's true nature. Moreover, most of the historical evil perpetrated on humanity by the church and the justifications for them can be attributed to unwillingness of Christians to "choose ye this day whom you shall serve." Will it be the God of your fathers (the God of Abraham, Isaac, and Jacob) or will it be God as Jesus has clearly defined him? Resolving this basic contradiction will require Christians to accept Jesus as the only authority on God and his true nature; and his true relationship with all humanity—a perfect father whose love for us is unconditional!

15

True Believers

There are two very important stories in the Bible about the power of simple belief in Jesus and his instructions regarding our ability to be successful healers. There was a man, whose name we do not know, who became a true disciple of Christ. I call him a true disciple because he integrated Jesus's teachings into his life and began to manifest God in the world by teaching and healing as he and the disciples had been instructed by Jesus. He went out and began to do the "greater works" just as Jesus said he should. But John complained to Jesus about the man saying, "Master we saw one casting out devils in thy name, and he followeth not us: and we forbad him, because he followeth not us" (Mark 9:38).

Implied in John's remark was that the disciples were an exclusive group (the new church and religion), and this man was not a member of that group. He was probably thinking, "Who does he think he is, that he can go about healing and casting out demons in Jesus's name? We did not give him permission or authority to do this!" Jesus's response to John and to the modern church was "Forbid him not: for there is no man which shall do a miracle in my name, that can lightly speak evil of me. For he that is not against us is on our part" (Mark 9:39–40).

However, the disciples should have been focusing on a more important issue than the ones they were concerned about. They should have been trying to figure out why this man was a more effective healer than they were. And we should be asking a more intriguing question: how was this man able to learn to heal the sick and cast out demons, when he barely spent enough time with Jesus for them to know his name? Even the disciples had trouble casting out demons. Yet this unnamed man could. If we can figure out the answer to this question, perhaps we can discover something quite important about the necessary conditions for successful healing. All that we know is that he attended at least one of Jesus's teaching and healing seminars. He believed what Jesus was teaching and followed his instructions. He watched how Jesus did it (heal the sick and cast out demons) and simply went out and duplicated Jesus's works.

The other remarkable story concerning the possibilities of ordinary human beings learning to do extraordinary things is found in the tenth chapter of Luke: "After these things the Lord appointed seventy also, and sent them two and two before his face into every city and place, wither he himself would come. Therefore said he unto them, 'The harvest truly is great, but the labourers are few: pray ye therefore the Lord of the harvest, that he would send forth labourers unto his harvest. Go your ways…and heal the sick that are therein, and say unto them, 'The kingdom of God is come nigh unto you'" (Luke 10:1–3, 9).

All we know about these men is that they were given instructions and a charge from Jesus to go on a healing mission. But the report suggests that they were able to master Jesus's instructions concerning the basic principles of healing to a degree that the disciples were unable to do. This is their most excellent report: "And the seventy returned again with joy, saying, 'Lord, even the devils are subject unto us through thy name'" (Luke 10:17).

How can we explain why these ordinary men, and probably ordinary women, were able to understand the seemly complex information that Jesus gave them concerning the power of God within them to perform miracles? How did they learn to draw on this power and successfully duplicate Jesus's work when the disciples did not learn this? What happened to this important knowledge that is so desperately needed in the modern church? The simple answer is that those who were successful believed everything Jesus taught them about God, himself, and themselves. They had faith in Jesus's teachings about all things and did not doubt.

I believe that it is possible for us to master the information and techniques of healing in the same manner as these anonymous men did. Nevertheless, learning how to heal and to routinely do miracles will require that we make a close and objective analysis of our current doctrines and theologies to determine the degree of harmony they have with both the spirit and letter of Jesus's gospel. Every contradiction must be resolved so that a sound theological basis for inspiring and teaching faith can be developed. Every false teaching about God's true nature must be eliminated in order to neutralize doubt and unbelief.

16

Lost Knowledge

These early Christians, the unnamed healer and the seventy, learned something from Jesus's teachings that the disciples did not grasp and most in the modern church have not learned. They learned how to do the "greater works" that Jesus did (miracles of healings and casting out demons). This knowledge concerning the ability to consistently heal the sick and cast out demons appears to have been lost. I believe it is safe to assume that there are no reliable miracles of healing in the modern-day church. *We have lost the knowledge and the ability to perform miracles of healing because our theology is based on what Luke has identified as the Apostles' Doctrine rather than a theology based on the gospel of Jesus Christ*

It is evident from the biblical record that Jesus must have given the disciples the same information about the fundamental principles of healing as he had given to the seventy. If these directives had not been given by Jesus in a very clear and understandable form, then neither the unnamed healer nor the seventy could have possibly healed the sick or cast out demons in the same manner that Jesus did. The scripture confirms the fact that the disciples had trouble casting out demons:

> "And when he came to his disciples, he saw a great multitude about them, and the scribes questioning with them…And he asked the scribes, 'What question ye them?' And one of the multitude answered and said, 'Master, I have brought unto thee my son, which has a dumb spirit; And wheresoever he taketh him, he teareth him: and he foameth, and gnasheth with his teeth, and pineth away: and I spake to thy disciples that they should cast him out; and they could not'" (Mark 9:14, 16–18).

The disciples could not cast out demons, but the unnamed healer and the seventy could. I will call this man and the seventy the "un-Thomases" because we know that they did not doubt. They had absolute confidence and belief in Jesus and his teachings; faith in themselves (Jesus said that anything I can do, you can do); and faith in the value and worth of all of those who were healed through their efforts. Jesus taught them to give up judgment and simply focus, as Jesus did in his life and ministry, on doing the "will of he who sent me."

First and foremost, these healers accepted Jesus's divinity and his authority! They obviously believed his gospel and apparently made a decision to follow Jesus's instructions to the letter for establishing and maintaining the psychological and spiritual conditions that make healing possible. This unnamed healer and the seventy were able to convince the people who came to them for healing about the truth of what they had seen Jesus do; and to persuade and inspire them that healing was possible because of what they heard Jesus say and because of what they had witnessed with their very eyes!

The world may have taught them that they were sinners and unworthy of anything from God. But Jesus taught them that everyone was a child of God, and that God, the perfect Father had a parental *obligation* to supply all of their needs. They may have been taught that there were diseases that medical science of their day could not cure. Nevertheless, Jesus taught them about a power that "could move a mountain" and that by the power of faith, any sickness or disease would be healed. Jesus also assured the seventy and the unnamed healer, in the same manner in which he assured the disciples and every Christian today, that we shall do the greater works. It is apparent that the seventy and this unnamed man believed what Jesus taught them in a way that the disciples nor modern day Christians could not or will not believe.

Modern-day Christians must take on the attributes of "the seventy" and the "unnamed man" if we are to become successful healers. To do this, we must be willing to give up our unwavering commitment to false doctrines and ideologies that are not reflective of Jesus's teachings. We most consider the full implications of the dialogue between Jesus and the lawyer: "'Master, which is the great commandment in the law?' Jesus said unto him, 'Thou shall love the Lord thy God with all thy heart, and with all thy soul, and with all thy mind. This is the first and great commandment. And the second is like unto it, Thou shall love thy neighbour as thy self" (Matt. 22:36–40).

Therefore the first step in learning to be a successful and reliable healer is to understand that it all begins with love of God, love of self, and love for each other. And to be certain that we did not misunderstand what Jesus was saying about what God commands us to do, he said to the disciples and to us, "A new commandment I give unto you, That ye love one another; as I have loved you, that ye also love one another. By this shall all men know that ye are my disciples, if ye have love one for another" (John 13:34–35).

Love is not an abstract theoretical concept. It is a living reality that must be expressed behaviorally on a daily basis. Love has been defined as an intense affection for another person or a group based on familial or personal ties. All of those in need of healing are your brothers and sisters. Remember: Jesus's teachings and his behavior are the model for the attributes, attitudes, and behavior of the modern-day Christian healer. We have been instructed by Jesus to love one another as he has loved us. But a close examination of the record in the Acts of the Apostles illustrates quite clearly that the disciples did not understand Jesus's concept of love. Moreover, history is a witness that the vast majority of Christians did not and still do not understand what Jesus was trying to teach the world about the true meaning of divine love. Because we do not understand Jesus's concept of love, our abilities to generate healing faith in any of our brothers and sisters are fatally compromised.

17

The Role of Faith in the Healing Process

Most of the traditional definitions of faith fail to capture the true sense of what the concept means as Jesus describes it. In a biblical dictionary, faith is defined as trust or reliance on God. It has also been defined as a strong belief and complete trust in someone or something. Faith, according to another definition, is a confident belief in the truth, value, or trustworthiness of a person, idea, or thing. Yet, there is another definition that I believe may capture a little more of the essence of the term. Faith is simply a focused and repetitious thought coupled with belief.

Belief, then, is the mental act of placing confidence in a person or thing. Another aspect of belief is the acceptance of the truth or being convicted of the validity of a person or a thing. Unbelief then is the rejection of the validity of a person or thing or the lack of confidence therein. There is ample evidence in the Bible of the difficulties the disciples had with faith and unbelief. Some of the problems modern Christians have with faith are related to the eternal conflict between "flesh," or the world of nature and science, and "spirit," or the world of God and the kingdom of God. Then, there are the enduring problems related to the contradictions between our theologies and Jesus's teachings.

The following report will provide a classic example of how the conflicts between the Word (Jesus) and theology influence our understanding of concepts such as faith and unbelief. Jesus provided a graphic demonstration of the power of thought, the spoken word (thoughts made manifest), and faith (power of belief):

> "And seeing a fig tree afar off having leaves, he came, if haply he might find any thing thereon: and when he came to it, he found nothing but leaves; for the time of figs was not yet. And Jesus answered and said unto it, 'No man eat fruit of thee hereafter for ever.' And his disciples heard it…And in the morning, as they passed by, they saw the fig tree dried up from the root. And Peter

calling to remembrance said unto him, 'Master, behold, the fig tree which thou cursedst is withered away'" (Mark 11:13–14, 20–21).

However, in one biblical reference book, the interpretation of this particular section of scripture is: "The cursing of the fig tree is explained by the fact that the fruit of this tree appears before the leaves, and a tree so full of leaves indicates that ripe figs should be there, even though it was not yet the regular season. The meaning is then, that when one has an outward show of a good character without its fruits, he is but a hypocrite and no value to the kingdom of God" (Cruden's Complete Concordance: pp 217.)

This is a classic example of how a theological interpretation of Jesus's teachings distorts the basic meaning and purpose of the instructions. I believe that these distortions are made to support a consistent and seamless theology or doctrine rather than the truth of what Jesus taught. It is also a prime example of how the disciples and modern-day Christians miss the true messages contained in Jesus's life and his teachings. Jesus continues the dialogue in this passage, and makes a very profound point about faith and healing. In reply to Peter's observation that the tree was dead, the scripture reports: "Jesus answering saith unto them, 'Have faith in God. For verily I say unto you that whosoever shall say unto this mountain, 'Be thou removed, and thou be cast unto the sea;' and shall not doubt in his heart, but shall believe that those things which he saith shall come to pass; he shall have whatever he saith. Therfore I say unto you, what things soever ye desire, when ye pray, believe that ye receive them, and ye shall have them'" (Mark 11:22–24).

This particular fig tree served as a *teaching aid* employed by Jesus to illustrate the power of thought, words, and belief. According to Jesus's instructions, miracles of healing are possible if we can generate an infinitely small amount of faith or belief, eliminate doubt, and pray for whatever we desire. Jesus says quite clearly "what things so ever ye desire when ye pray...ye shall have it." This basic lesson suggests to us that there is enough real power in an amount of faith that is almost too small to see to literally move a mountain.

Jesus reemphasizes the points I have previously made about both the power of faith and the power of unbelief in another situation involving a man with a son who was possessed by a demon. This event occurred after the transfiguration, and Jesus's time with the disciples was growing short; the crucifixion was just beyond the horizon. The scripture relates:

"When they were come to the multitude, there came a certain man, kneeling down to him, and saying, 'Lord, have mercy on my son: for he is lunatic, and sore vexed: for ofttimes he falleth into the fire, and oft into water. And I brought him to thy disciples, and they could not cure him.' Then Jesus answered and said, 'O faithless and perverse generation, how long shall I be with you? How long shall I suffer you? Bring him hither to me.' And Jesus rebuked the devil; and he departed out of him: and the child was cured from that hour. Then came the disciples to Jesus apart, and said, 'Why could we not cast him out?' And Jesus said unto them, 'Because of your unbelief: for verily I say unto you, if you have faith as a grain of mustard seed, ye shall say unto this mountain, "Remove hence to yonder place" and it shall remove and nothing shall be impossible unto you'" (Matt. 17:14–20).

Again, Jesus confronts the disciples about their unbelief. We have seen that unbelief, caused by confusion in the minds of the people of Nazareth about Jesus's identity (Son of God or son of Joseph?), was powerful enough to stifle Jesus's ability to do great works there (Matt. 13:58). But Jesus told his disciples and all Christians, that there is enough real spiritual power in an amount of faith you can barely see with the naked eye to literally move a mountain—all by the spoken word powered by faith or belief.

The healer, then, must understand what Jesus is saying and believe it in order to help those in need of healing momentarily release whatever doubt they may hold in their hearts and teach them to believe. If this is accomplished, healing becomes possible. The seventy and the unnamed healer learned this from Jesus in a way that the disciples did not and that we have not yet been able to master.

Paul, who seemed to have had more wisdom and understanding about Jesus and what he was trying to teach us than the disciples, gives us the following important observation about how faith is generated: "So, then faith cometh by hearing, and hearing by the word of God" (Rom. 10:17). Paul did not say that faith came by words—his or that of the disciples, patriarchs, prophets, or scribes. He said that faith comes by the words of God. Jesus has clearly stated that he is the *only voice for God,* and he commands us to "repent ye, and believe the gospel" (Mark 1:15). It is important to remember that to repent in this context means to change your mind or your way of thinking.

The healer then must study all of the information Jesus has given us about healing. He or she must also examine all of the stories about healing in the four Gospels and the descriptive circumstances in which they occurred. All of this information must be integrated into a believable narrative that can be told to an audience in much the same manner as the unnamed healer or the seventy must have reported Jesus's message or "words of God" to the people they healed. The healer must also be aware that in many places, elements of the Apostles' Doctrine have been carefully woven into Jesus's messages.

It is important for us to understand that faith can be generated today the same way it was generated in the past by the seventy and the unnamed healer. Faith comes by telling people the stories about God and Jesus in their respective roles as perfect father and miracle-working healer. The major themes of these stories should be about our heavenly Father's unconditional love for us and his faithful devotion to us and what Jesus said was required to get whatever you need from God: simply ask and believe!

We must also tell the stories about Jesus, the Word made flesh, who came to manifest God to us in unmistakable ways through his teaching and his miracles of healing. We should add stories about the miracles of healing we have experienced and seen with our own eyes. The sole purpose should be to communicate the basic message Jesus gave us that "whatsoever you ask in my name, I will do it." We who profess to know Jesus should be willing and able to do this! A casual observation of any Sunday morning church service will show that the major focus of the overwhelming number of sermons are on issues of repentance, as our doctrines and ideologies have defined this concept, rather than on healing. Thus we have continued to miss the message.

18

The Healing Lessons

I have described some of my early healing experiences because of the underlying lessons inherent in these experiences. My belief is that God gives every Christian the ability to heal as an expression of his unconditional love for us. The only expectation is that we will share it unconditionally with anyone God sends to us for healing. The Holy Spirit will give a sign that the purpose of the encounter is to share a gift of healing.

What the ex-nun, the Jewish atheist, the homosexual supervisor, and the young "backsliding" woman I talked about earlier had in common was that they all were out of fellowship with traditional Christian doctrines. According to our religious beliefs and standards, they were unrepentant sinners. Yet, God granted each of them a miracle of healing as an expression of unconditional love for them and for me. It also proved that God takes his divine parental responsibilities for us seriously. I had sufficient faith that healing was possible because of things I know to be true about Jesus and God, based on the information Jesus gave us. In summary, Jesus taught us:

- Our father in heaven is a perfect father (Matt. 5:48).

- We can do the "greater works" (miracles/healing), if we believe on him (John 14:12).

- Whatever we ask in Jesus's name, he will do it (John 14:14).

- We have the power to do miracles in us (John 14:20).

- There is sufficient power in a small amount of faith to get anything we need from God (Matt. 17:20, Luke 17:6).

- God treats all of his children equally and gives life's necessities to all regardless of behavior (Matt. 5:45).

- God loves all of his children unconditionally (John 3:16).

- The Holy Spirit will direct you in any potential healing encounters.

- You should never judge anyone because you do not know enough about him or her or about their true relationship with God to make a judgment about them.

- The only truth you should be aware of is that *all* are children of God who are equally loved by him! (Matt. 5:45–48; John 3:16; John 13:34–35).

During the Sermon on the Mount, Jesus makes it very clear to us that God wants us to love everyone in the same way God loves all of his children. Jesus also characterizes God as a "perfect Father." Sun and rain are metaphors for the life-sustaining essentials. God, our perfect Father, provides these essentials for both his good and his evil children, as well as to his just and unjust ones (Matt. 5:45).

Using the analogy of human parents, if a wayward child contracted a serious illness, no expense would be spared to heal or save them. Moreover, no one would ever question if this "sinful or bad child" deserved to be healed. We would never even suggest that there would be any conditions placed on the child's healing other than the need for a cure. Furthermore, should anyone suggest the child did not deserve healing because of something the child had done, a human parent would reject that notion, knowing that the person making it truly did not understand what Jesus was trying to teach us about God. There would also never be any suggestion of conditions the child had to meet before we would fulfill our parental obligation to provide or care for them.

We would find the best medical treatment and most skillful doctors for the child and would fervently pray to God that the child would be healed. Jesus said, "If you, being evil, know how to give good gifts unto your children, how much more shall your father, which is in heaven, give good things to them that ask him?" (Matt. 7:11). The information about God's love and responsibilities for all of his children must be written on our hearts in an indelible and powerful way so that we can teach it with certainty to all who are in need of healing.

19

Integrating Healing in Your Christian Life

The awareness of your inherent abilities to heal should be in your thoughts at all times. Moreover the Holy Spirit, who is your link to Jesus and the power of God, is ready and able to perform miracles on your behalf. To be a successful healer, you must first believe that what Jesus says about God is true, and that Jesus, according to his word, is the only biblical authority on God (John 6:19–47). You must also believe in yourself as valued and worthy in the sight of God. Furthermore, you must know your status and relationship with God at all times. You are the holy child of a perfect father who loves you unconditionally, and because of his unchanging nature and faithfulness, your father is ever mindful of your needs and the obligations to fulfill them (Matt. 6:25–34).

You cannot suggest, in any manner, that God will not honor his obligations to meet the needs of his children based on your concepts of sin or righteousness. Jesus said that the only conditions for healing are to ask and to believe. You must believe this, and in case you forget, remind yourself of this truth frequently. Your abilities to consistently do miracles of healing are dependent upon how well you understand this. And you can only teach this if you know this is a certainty from the depths of your being.

The conditions for self-healing are created through a process that takes place in the mind and the spirit. In the story of the fig tree (Mark 11), Jesus had an idea in his mind about the most dramatic way to demonstrate the truth of a reality that most of us are unaware of. So he decided to use an innocent fig tree to teach all of humanity an important lesson about the critical role thoughts and words play in creating our realities.

After finding no fruit on the tree, he cursed it, and it died overnight. When Peter noticed that the fig tree had died, he was shocked and surprised. In response to Peter's comment about the dead tree, Jesus said, "Have faith in God" (Mark

11:22). So the first lesson was that there is real power in a thought and its expression by the spoken word. There is also real power in faith or belief because doubt and unbelief are equally powerful in the prevention of healing. To heal yourself, you must focus your attention on the positive intent to receive a gift of healing from the Father who promised you that you are entitled to healing. Focus continually on healing!

The reality is that all thoughts have power. What you think consistently will eventually come to pass. So, to initiate a healing process two things must happen in the mind: faith in what Jesus taught about healing must be established in your thinking (and doubt must be neutralized) and a strong intent to be healed must be generated and maintained.

To increase your faith in what Jesus taught, remember the stories of faith in the Bible and repeat them to yourself. Repeatedly read the scriptures quoted in this book. Remember all of the miracles of healing and deliverance you have seen and heard about, and continue to believe and know that you are worthy and entitled to have what you need. Thus to be able to heal conditions requiring a miracle, ask your perfect Father in the name of Jesus for healing, believe that you shall have it, and you will!

Creating a strong intent to be healed is the second condition. Intent is defined in Webster's Dictionary as having the mind, attention, or will centered on something or some end or purpose. An intention to be healed is concentrated attention on being healed or made whole. The focus is not on being sick, it is on being healed. Think only thoughts of being healed.

The healing chain of thoughts is created in the following way. As we discussed earlier, Luke reported the following healings in the early stages of Jesus's ministry.

> "Now when he came nigh to the gate of the city, behold, there was a dead man carried out, the only son of his mother, and she was a widow: and much people of the city was with her. And when the Lord saw her, he had compassion on her, and said unto her, 'Weep not.' And he came and touched the bier: and they that bare him stood still. And he said, "Young man, I say unto you, Arise.' And he that was dead sat up and begin to speak. And he delivered him to his mother. And there came a fear on all: and they glorified God, saying, 'That a great prophet is risen up among us; and God hath visited his people.' And the rumour of him went forth throughout all Judaea, and throughout all regions round about (Luke 7:12–17).

As the rumors of Jesus spread, a chain of intent to be healed began to develop among the people. They went beyond believing it was possible and sought Jesus.

When Jesus came down from the mountain, great multitudes followed him. But a leper found him a place along the route and fell down and worshipped Jesus, saying "Lord if thou wilt, thou canst make me clean." And Jesus put forth his hand and touched him saying, "I will; be thou clean" Immediately, his leprosy was cleansed (Luke 5:12–13). On another occasion, Jesus was in Samaria. When he went to a village, ten lepers stood off from the crowd and cried out, "Jesus, Master, have mercy on us." When he saw them, he told them to go show themselves to the priests. "And it came to pass, that, as they went, they were cleansed" (Luke 17:11–14). They came to the place where Jesus was with the intention of being healed and their faith or belief made them whole.

Then, there was a woman with an issue of blood, who heard that Jesus was coming down a particular road. When she got there, there was a crowd of people so dense that she could not get to the roadside: "And a certain woman, which had an issue of blood twelve years, and had suffered many things of many physicians, and had spent all that had, and was nothing bettered but rather grew worse, when she heard of Jesus, came in the press behind, and touched his garment. For she said, 'If I may touch his clothes, I shall be whole.' And straightway the fountain of her blood was dried up; and she felt in her body that she was healed of that plague" (Mark 5:25–29).

She heard that Jesus, the healer, was coming. Therefore, she pressed her way through the crowd to get to him. Her focus was on Jesus and healing. This woman did not let the failures and disappointments of the physicians deter her from her healing nor did she permit the crowd to hinder her. Neither did the two blind men at Jericho (Matt. 20:30) nor blind Bartimaeus (Mark 10:46) let the opinions of the crowds deter them from calling out to Jesus for their healing.

Everyone who came to Jesus for healing was healed. They came with a strong expectation that Jesus would heal them based on the stories they had heard from others. Jesus promised us that anything he did, we could do. But to be healed, you must overcome the vast clouds of doubt (thoughts based on false beliefs about God) and the witnesses of the world who talk and act as if there are some things too hard for God or suggest that God's obligations and responsibilities for his children are conditional upon the children's behavior. Therefore, believe what Jesus said about you, God, and your relationship with him. Never forget that God has parental obligations and real responsibilities for all of his children. Ask for a healing for yourself or for a loved one. Ask, believing!

Moreover, be a witness. Develop a narrative based on your favorite stories from the reports in the Bible about Jesus's many miracles of healing. Integrate your own stories and the stories of reliable witnesses who have experienced miracles of healing from God. Repeat your story to yourself. Talk faith with each other. Inspire faith and belief! Cast out doubt and unbelief! Then healing will come.

Permit me to digress a moment and share with you a powerful miracle of healing in my own life. As I mentioned, after the death of my father when I was almost four, it became necessary for my mother and the two older siblings to leave the household to work. The trauma of my father's death and the destabilization of the household precipitated an intense depressive neurosis with acute anxiety and chronic insomnia. These conditions grew progressively worse, and by the time I was in my middle twenties, I was taking prescription medications to control these conditions and was addicted to alcohol.

About the same time that God directed me to AA, my mother called Unity's twenty-four-hour prayer line and requested prayer for me. They sent her a short prayer to give to me. The prayer simply said *"I let the love of God flow through me, calming my emotions, freeing my mind, and healing my body."*

I committed this prayer to memory and repeated it every waking minute of every day. If I had to focus on something related to work, commuting, or at an AA meeting, I would focus. When anxious thoughts began to surface, I would immediately switch my focus to prayer and God. Within a year, the depression, anxiety, and sleep disorder were healed. I have shared this prayer with hundreds of other clients who have achieved similar results in healing conditions that medical science has difficulties treating.

Therefore, pray in a simple, straightforward manner. God is your perfect father who loves you unconditionally. You can talk to him in the same manner you would speak to an earthly father whom you loved and who loved you. Speak to God, not begging or uncertain but boldly and confidently as Paul suggested when he said: "Let us therefore come boldly unto the throne of grace that we may obtain mercy and find grace to help in times of need" (Heb. 4:16).

20

The Theology of a Healing Ministry

Jesus did not say our abilities to heal depended on believing the Apostles' Doctrine or any other doctrine created by man. He said that we should believe on him, his teachings, and his examples. A new theology of healing based on Jesus's gospel is desperately needed in these modern times. Moreover, I believe that the modern-day Christian church has an obligation to develop such a theology.

When Jesus dispatched the seventy men on their healing mission, he told them, "The harvest truly is great, but the labourers are few: Pray ye therefore the Lord of the harvest, that he would send forth labourers into his harvest" (Luke 10:2). Jesus's observations are as true now as they were in his day because the sick, troubled, and diseased are still with us. Overwhelming numbers of them are either in our churches or have grown up in a church. Nevertheless, our sermons and ministries have not been able to draw them and keep them. Nor have we been able to heal them with any degree of consistency

Every Christian knows something about Jesus and his miracle-working powers, and have some ideas about God. In the three years of Jesus's ministry, he established a reputation as a teacher and healer that spread throughout Israel, Judea, and Samaria (Matt. 4:24–25; Luke 7:17). But after three hundred years of preaching and teaching, the followers of Christ were still a small but persecuted sect. It was only through the conversion of the Roman Emperor Constantine's wife and the subsequent joining of the early Christian church with the power of the secular state that Christianity began to spread in the western world. The moving power in the spread of Christianity was the might of the Roman army. Men were not drawn to the church through the power of Jesus's gospel and God's love but by the power of fear and intimidation. It is time, I believe, for the church to recreate itself in the image of Christ through a ministry of healing based on unconditional love.

A ministry of healing is a ministry of love. Jesus said that if we make him, his teachings, and his example the center of our Christian life, that he would draw all men unto himself! I believe that a ministry in your church devoted strictly to healing will be successful. Moreover, the success we shall have by inspiring miracles of healing in the name of Jesus will serve as a powerful light that will draw men and women closer to Christ in a way that our most powerful sermons are unable to do.

The goal of this ministry should be to heal so that all will know God, in the form of his mighty healing power, is being manifested among us. The message should be that healing is the gift that God has given to the world through us, as a living testimony of his faithfulness and love. Healing in the name of Jesus is also a way of glorifying the Father in the Son. Let me cite one additional example of the power of faith and trust in the healing process.

In the book of Numbers, we have the continuing story of the faithlessness of the children of Israel in their trust in the Father. God had delivered them out of bondage, working many mighty miracles. The record illustrates that as soon as the next crisis arose, they became discouraged, rebellious, and began to doubt. On one occasion, when they began to speak against God and complaining to Moses, God sent a plague of poisonous serpents among them. Everyone who was bitten died. When the people repented and asked Moses to pray to God to remove the serpents, the word states: "And the Lord said unto Moses, 'Make thee a fiery serpent, and set it upon a pole: and it shall come to pass, that every one that is bitten, when he looketh upon it, shall live.' And Moses made a serpent of brass, and put it upon a pole, and it came to pass, that if a serpent had bitten any man, when he beheld the serpent of brass, he lived" (Num. 21:8–9).

This passage is about faith and healing. But it is also an illustration of the reality of where the power to heal is to be found. There was no inherent power in the "brazen serpent" to heal. Looking up was an act of faith that triggered the healing power. Jesus reminds us when he states, "At that day ye shall know that I am in my Father, and ye in me, and I in you" (John 14:20). Jesus is saying that all of the power of creation is in us. If we believe what Jesus is saying, we can invoke this power through prayer and faith. Thus Jesus reminds us that something important happens when we look to him above all things. He said to us, "And as Moses lifted up the serpent in the wilderness, even so must the Son of man be lifted up" (John 3:14).

The theologians have interpreted this passage as a reference to the crucifixion. My contention is that "lifting up the serpent" is about an act of faith and healing. Everyone who looked up received a miracle of healing and deliverance from certain physical death. One interpretation we can make of Jesus's words is (1) let them see Jesus in you, (2) put them in touch with Jesus in them, and (3) inspire hope and trust in God, and in his love and his power. Then healing will come. Lift up Jesus so all can see him! And all things are possible.

21

Becoming an Effective Christian Healer

If any Christians (pastors, ministers, evangelists, lay church members, etc.) want to develop the ability to be an effective healer, they must be willing to master the necessary spiritual concepts and skills needed to become a reliable healer, as Jesus has taught and demonstrated them in his healing ministry. One must also be willing to give up some treasured ideas, beliefs, and practices that are contrary to Jesus's basic teachings. For example, Christians have historically believed that there are justifications for wars and killings. Many traditional Christians believe in the death penalty. The Christian justification for killing in wars and putting "bad" people to death is the "eye for an eye, tooth for a tooth" edict in the Mosaic Law. This is one of the laws that Jesus repudiated in the Sermon on the Mount.

We tend to choose to follow the teachings and traditions of the Old Testament when it suits our purposes—owning slaves, killing people we have defined as enemies, subjugating women and children to male domination, imposing our religious beliefs and practices on others, for example. We forget that Jesus taught just the opposite. So, we are quite ready to ignore any of Jesus's basic teachings when we want to justify judgment, anger, violence, and unforgiveness. Moreover, we are quick to find scriptural justification for all of our unChristlike attitudes by quoting a biblical authority other than Jesus. Thus, we assign equal weight to every speaker in the Bible.

This is especially true as it relates to the great spiritual concepts like love, judgment, patience, tolerance, forgiveness, and the lack of justification for conflicts and violence. It is amazing that we so easily forget that Jesus said that his new commandment was that we love one another as he has loved us, and this would be the true sign that we were his disciples. The healer must know this and be able to demonstrate unconditional love in everything that is done and so be able to teach this principle to those in need of healing.

The ability to love others unconditionally is one of the first spiritual characteristics the healer must develop. By unconditional love, I am speaking about being willing and able to integrate the basic characteristic of love as the apostle Paul defined this concept in his first letter to the Corinthians or as Jesus manifested them in his day-to-day interactions with his brothers and sisters during his life and ministry. To develop this degree of love, the healer must give up judgment completely.

In the Sermon on the Mount, Jesus instructs us not to judge one another because we do not have enough knowledge to judge correctly. Every Christian tends to believe that they know the proper path to salvation and true worship. Most believe that their particular denomination is the true way. Jesus addressed this issue in a very unambiguous manner in his teaching session with the Samaritan woman.

Although Samaritans and Jews shared a common heritage, they were separated by religious beliefs and practices. As a religious sect, the Samaritans were a strict, Torah-observing people with great pride in their religious heritage. One of the major ideological beliefs separating them was the Jews' belief that Jerusalem and Mount Zion were sacred places sanctified by God and the only place where true worship was possible. The Samaritans believed that Mount Gerizim was the sacred place where God was to be worshipped. The Samaritans also had different legal traditions about the Mosaic Law. The Jews of Jesus's day hated Samaritans, thinking them unclean heretics who would surely go to hell. Perhaps it is the same intensity of prejudice and hatred as white Americans had for African Americans during the era of slavery and segregation.

What Jesus was trying to teach was that all of us have equal rights and favor with God. The religious division between Jews and Samaritans, and the prejudice and hatred generated by these divisions, are similar to that which exists today between Jews and Arabs, between Christians and non-Christians, and between fundamentalist Christians and others types of Christians judged to be somehow less holy and deserving of salvation.

This Samaritan woman, according to the Bible, had an unsavory reputation and was "living in sin." She raised an essential issue with Jesus about the nature of true worship when she asked who is right in the lingering conflict between Jews and Samaritans. She made a comment and asked, "'Our fathers worshipped in this mountain; and ye say that in Jerusalem is the place where men ought to worship.' Jesus said to her, 'Women, believe me, the hour cometh, when ye shall neither in this mountain, nor yet at Jerusalem, worship the Father. But the hour cometh and now is when the true worshippers shall worship the Father in spirit and in truth: for the Father seeketh such to worship him. God is a Spirit: and they that worship him must worship him in spirit and in truth'" (John 4:20–24).

Our belief that we know the right ways of worship have led to wars resulting in the death of thousands of our brothers and sisters. However, according to Jesus, what we think we know is really only our particular belief about salvation. We think that what we believe is true, but Jesus said that we are blind and cannot see. He did not qualify his statement. He simply said we have a beam (total blockage of sight) in our eye (Matt. 7:5).

Jesus demonstrated time and again that the Jew's judgments about Samaritans were false. Jesus's close and loving relationship with the Samaritans was a strong commentary of the love God had for this group of people whom the Jews had defined as an abomination in the sight of God. The message to the modern church is that unbelievers are as precious in the sight of God as true believers. God's love for his children is eternal and unconditional. There is no record that Jesus ever told or suggested to any Samaritan that God's love for them was less than his love for the Jews. He never suggested that there was anything they had to repent of other than to give up their mistaken notions about God's true nature and about what constitutes true worship.

It is important for us to remember that Jesus said "'I am the way, the truth and the life'" (John 14:6). A way is a path, a body of teachings, instructions, or a discipline. Truth is what has been demonstrated to be factual and life is the essence of our being or God in us. It is apparent that the unnamed healer and the seventy believed what Jesus said and understood what he was teaching to an extent that the disciples did not.

I say this because the records indicate that before the Crucifixion and Resurrection, before the fall of the Holy Ghost, and before the evolution of Christian theology, these nameless healers were empowered by Jesus to manifest God among us in the same manner as Jesus. They healed the sick and cast out demons. It is recorded, "And Jesus went about all of Galilee, teaching in their synagogues, and preaching the gospel of the kingdom, and healing all manner of sickness and all manner of disease among the people. And his fame went throughout all Syria: and they brought unto him all sick people that were taken with diverse diseases and torments, and those which were possessed with devils, and those who were lunatic, and those that had the palsy; and he healed them" (Matt. 4:23–24).

Much fear and anxiety will be relieved in this world when it is established that the sick and diseased are drawn to our churches because they believe we can heal them. However, to be an effective healer, the pastor or Christian leader must truly understand Jesus's teachings and instructions. His words must be written on our hearts and integrated into our minds. The willingness to believe and follow Jesus's instructions and example were major factors in the success of the unknown man as a reliable healer.

I also believe that true "mountain-moving faith" has been lost because Christians are not spiritually mature enough to be trusted not to abuse God's power in any way. Peter's use of the power and authority of the Holy Ghost to kill Ananias and Sapphira is a classic example of this type of spiritual immaturity. Thus, in order for us to regain the power to heal, we must give up judgment and the desire to punish those who do not believe as we do or act the way we think they ought to behave. Remember the Samaritans!

I believe that whatever successes I have had as a healer in the secular world have been possible because I resolved many of these contradictions about God's true nature and character. As Jesus said, our purpose in being here is to manifest God's love toward one another. I believe, with all of my mind and my heart, that manifesting the power of God in the world by faith through doing the work Jesus charged us to do is what constitutes "true worship."

The healer must be able to inspire faith and dispel unbelief in the minds of those in need of healing. Because the maintenance of faith is so difficult, many believe that there is something wrong with them or with their relationship with God because of the problems they have with their seeming lack of faith. However, the truth is, that all of us probably have a greater measure of faith than the disciples. According to the scriptures about the multiplication of the loaves the disciples' first response to every crisis was doubt or fear.

We would think that given the things they had seen him do, nothing Jesus did would have surprised them. But when they saw him walking on the water, they thought he was a ghost. Here is the logic of the ego or flesh mind: a ghost, which they had never seen but believe existed, could walk on water. Jesus, who had demonstrated that he was God manifested among them, could not do this. After all, a man walking on water violates all the laws of science and nature. This is the report:

> "But straightway Jesus spake unto them, saying, 'Be of good cheer; it is I; be not afraid.' And Peter answered him and said, 'Lord, if it be thou, bid me come unto thee on the water.' And he said, 'Come.' And when Peter was come down out of the ship, he walked on the water, to go to Jesus. But when he saw the wind boisterous, he was afraid; and beginning to sink, he cried, saying, 'Lord, save me.' And immediately Jesus stretched forth his hand, and caught him, and said unto him, 'O thou of little faith, wherefore didst thou doubt?'" (Matt. 14:27–31).

This is one of the many examples of the struggles the disciples had with their faith. I think the disciples and their followers tell these stories so that we can understand what a difficult task it is to generate and maintain faith and to control the tendency to doubt. What the healer must teach is that faith is difficult for us who have never seen Jesus. But by the same token, it was also difficult for the disciples who were with him and witnessed all of his mighty works.

Nevertheless, we should all be encouraged; it only takes a small amount of faith to move a mountain. Thus, it will only take an infinitesimal small amount of faith to get a miracle of healing. Faith comes by hearing and hearing comes by the word of God. The healer must have the ability to inspire faith in those in need of healing as well as dispel unbelief and doubt. This is our charge because successful healing depends on faith in God and faith in the promise made by Jesus Christ that whatsoever we ask in his name, "I will do it." Successful healing will also depend on the ability of the healer to define all of God's children, including themselves, as worthy and entitled to have whatever they need from their perfect father.

22

The Healing Environment

I have found that the spiritual retreat, faith-based workshop, or seminar format are the most effective structures in which to conduct a healing ministry because of the need to create a spiritual environment or atmosphere conducive to healing. These formats are also a statement that the healing session is not to be mistaken for church as usual. The record indicates that whenever Jesus was coming to a town or village, the people would gather all of the sick in one location with the expectation that Jesus would heal them all. So the healing service should be devoted solely to healing. The workshop or seminar format is appropriate because of the educational component. The content of the didactic component of the session will include the information and material discussed above. You will note that all of this material is scriptural in nature, and based exclusively on Jesus's teachings. I did not create any of the facts.

There is also an experiential component that will include stories about miracles of healing. The goal is to create an environment of faith that is powerful and intense enough for the majority of participants to expect a miracle of healing, no matter what the condition may be. I know we can do this because Jesus said, "'Verily I say unto you, Whatsoever ye shall bind on earth shall be bound in heaven: and whatsoever ye shall loose on earth shall be loosed in heaven. Again I say unto you, That if two of you shall agree on earth as touching any thing that they shall ask, it shall be done for them of my Father which is in heaven. For where two or three are gathered together in my name, there am I in the midst of them'" (Matt. 18:18–20).

The ministers of healing must be skilled at creating a warm, supportive, non-threatening spiritual environment with a total absence of judgment. We must try and understand what it was about Jesus's personality that was so attractive to the wide variety of people who mobbed him wherever he went. Then we must prayerfully try to take on these Christlike characteristics and manifest them in the environment. We are speaking of faith, hope, and compassion. We must also be able to create an atmosphere of confidence and expectation that nothing is too hard for God.

I create this environment by telling stories of healing from the Bible, relating these stories to Jesus's basic teachings about God as a perfect father and the implications of this for everyone in the room. I also teach about how judgment, anger, guilt, and shame affect our faith, trust, and confidence in God. I work diligently to keep everything I teach or say grounded in what Jesus taught or said. I know that the real power is not in what I think or say, but in what Jesus said. I know that whatever is accomplished is done by the power of the Word through the workings of the Spirit of God that dwells in each of us.

23

A Healing Ministry in Your Church?

Jesus often used the analogy of the good shepherd in defining his relationship with God's children. He stated that a good shepherd is always concerned about the physical safety and well-being of his flock. Jesus consistently provided healing for his flock, thus setting an example for modern-day shepherds to follow. He said that pastors and ministers, as shepherds of the flock who profess to believe on him, should be doing the greater works of miracles and healing on a routine basis. However, if you are a pastor and you are not utilizing the power of the Holy Ghost in attending to the healing needs of your congregation, you are not meeting your responsibilities as a good shepherd.

Anyone who feels they are called to heal and are willing to give up some of their cherished theological and doctrinal beliefs can master Jesus's healing methods and techniques. I have given a tremendous amount of thought about this gift God has given me and how it is to be used. I have debated whether the gift was to be used in the church or whether I should continue to do healing workshops in the secular world. After much prayer, I have been led to at least explore the possibility of developing a healing ministry in my church. So I developed a proposal for developing a healing ministry in my church.

Another factor in writing the initial proposal for developing a healing ministry in our church is related to a set of circumstances that have evolved over the past few years. My pastor was elevated to Bishopric and the Office of Jurisdictional Prelate over about a hundred churches. He is a very Christlike pastor in many ways and I have tremendous respect for him. He is open to new ideas that are scriptural and theologically sound. If the concept of a separate healing ministry is successful in our church, we can replicate the model throughout the jurisdiction. Moreover, because COGIC is a world church, there is the potential for a healing revival throughout the land.

I have tried to analyze the relationship between my basic beliefs about God and my abilities to be an effective instrument of healing. The above narrative contains the scriptural basis for these beliefs and the manner in which these beliefs affect the issues of my faith in God and the ability to heal. As I have stated, I believe that it is possible to understand what Jesus taught about healing. I also believe that an objective reading of the scripture will validate my basic premises that (a) healing was an essential aspect of Jesus's ministry; (b) Jesus's intent was that the church should continue this aspect of his ministry; (c) Jesus gave us instructions on healing; (d) they can be taught; (e) a reliable healing ministry can be developed; (f) by focusing on Jesus's basic message we can develop a sound theological foundation for a healing ministry.

Finally, healing faith can be generated and doubt neutralized only if there are no contradictions being taught or expressed about God's unconditional love and his willingness to heal any of his children who are in need simply by "asking and believing." *The rituals of salvation, or giving your life to Christ (being saved) is not a prerequisite for healing.* If this was the case, none among the "saved and sanctified" or the righteous in our churches would be suffering from sicknesses and diseases.

Those who choose to become healers should focus closely on the Sermon on the Mount to gain some understanding of what God requires of the healer behaviorally. It is a series of generalized instructions on what a true follower of Christ must learn about how God would have us relate to each other. These instructions are designed to aid us in mastering the spiritual concepts of infinite patience, infinite tolerance, unconditional love, nonjudgment, and forgiveness. He is also teaching us that conflict, and its precursor, anger, cannot be justified under any circumstance because of its destructive influence on the mind and spirit.

The entire Gospel of John has essential information about God and his true nature. This gospel should be studied carefully and thoroughly. You must remember that some of the Apostles' Doctrine has been integrated into Jesus's gospel as doctrinal justification for the new religion and as justification for their behavior. My belief, based on Jesus's statement that "God is a Spirit: and they that worship him must worship in spirit and in truth" (John 4:24), is that creating another religion was not his primary purpose in coming here. He came to teach us the truth about God and about ourselves and how we are to treat one another.

The purpose of gaining mastery of this information is not to convince others of the truth of your belief system but simply to open up your understanding of what Jesus is teaching so that you can be a more effective Christian. The goal is to become like the unnamed healer or one of the seventy, who became healers of the same magnitude as Jesus. Study Jesus's words and integrate his teachings into your mind, spirit, and being. And believe his gospel. The charge from Jesus is to "Let your light so shine before men, that they may see your good works, and glorify your Father which is in heaven" (Matt. 5:16).

The church community is often referred to as the Body of Christ. Jesus defined himself as the kingdom of God. And in his being was all the knowledge of God, all of God's love, and all of his majesty and power. All of these godly attributes should be found in the church if the claim to be the Body of Christ is to be realized. A successful healing ministry will validate God's love, power, and faithfulness to his children and to his word in a way that our doctrines and theologies have been unable to do.

Miracles of healing should be natural to all of the children of God who have been created in our father's image and likeness. I pray to God that by the Spirit of the living God and the power of the Holy Ghost, we are able to develop a place in Christianity where any individual can come for healing. Through healing they will certainly know that "the kingdom of God is come nigh into you" (Luke 10:9).

In commenting about the need for healing in the world, Jesus said, "The harvest truly is great, but the labourers are few: pray ye therefore the Lord of the harvest, that he would send forth labourers into the harvest" (Luke 10:2). The idea that we can be "the labourers" sent by the Lord of the harvest in response to Jesus's prayer is an exciting possibility to me. I pray God that you may be able to establish a healing ministry in your church or ministry. I know that should you do it, God will bless your ministry in a powerful way. Healing is a work that generates a powerful light, and through healing in his name, Jesus is lifted up in such a way that men are drawn to him.

I know that some of the things I am proposing may be radical in nature and troubling to many Christians. Jesus said, however, for each of us to "repent ye, and believe the gospel" (Mark 1:15). Some would suggest that what I say borders on blasphemy or heresy. However, I am encouraging every Christian who reads this book to take a deep breath and "be still" for a moment. Consider the following: I have not said anything that is not based on scriptures or factual history. The challenge is to use the power of your Christian beliefs to inspire faith not in my words, but in Jesus's basic teachings that God is a God of unconditional love, prepared to meet all of the needs of his children.

Because one of the needs in this current day and time is for miracles of healing, I believe that it is our responsibility to develop healing ministries based on Jesus's teachings. To do this successfully, we must develop the abilities to teach faith and to neutralize guilt and unbelief in our beloved brothers and sisters. Learn to inspire "mountain-moving faith" by being a true witness of a loving Christ who will never change. Inspire belief in God who is our perfect Father as Jesus has taught us. Give up the Apostles' Doctrine and all the theological and doctrinal beliefs that are not reflective of Jesus's basic teachings. Give up judgment and practice unconditional love.

However, if you are uncomfortable with revising your current theology or dogma in the ways that I have suggested, you can develop an effective healing ministry without any real theological or doctrinal changes. In most churches, the main sermon is generally developed around a particular theme. The objectives of the sermon of the day will determine the theme and the supportive scripture. If the theme of the message is the eternal consequence of sin and the certainty of hell if you do not repent; then all of the scriptural references will reflect the theme. The main character in this particular drama will be the God of Abraham, Isaac, and Jacob or the punitive God of the Old Testament and all the stories of Sodom and Gomorrah, David and the Philistines, and Elijah and Jezebel and Ahab. Sermons of this nature, presented by a skilled and inspiring preacher will convince many "sinners" to repent.

On the next Sunday, the same skilled and inspiring preacher may decide to bring the message of God's faithfulness and unconditional love. Then the focus of the sermon will be on God the perfect Father of whom Jesus speaks. The supportive scriptures will be taken from Jesus's stories about God our perfect father. We will hear about the Prodigal Son, about Ruth and Naomi, and about Jesus, Mary, Martha and Lazarus. And if the sermon is preached with inspiration and power the entire congregation will know and feel God's enduring love and be convinced that this love is unconditional.

Now I will ask a rhetorical question. Should not a skilled minister or pastor be able to develop and preach a sermon that will inspire sufficient faith in God that miracles of healing become possible? However, to preach such a sermon, there cannot be any contradictory material in the sermon that may create doubt and unbelief. The key to miracles of healing in you church is to develop a healing sermon and present it on a regular basis. *God will not mind if you postpone the "fire and brimstone" for a later date. Jesus, I believe will be pleased that you are willing to devote a few of your Sunday mornings to his favorite ministry; a ministry of healing!* Focus on miracles of healing exclusively as the theme of the service and the Holy Spirit will honor you church with a successful healing ministry where miracles are the norm rather than the exception.

24

Conclusions

If you are a pastor of a church, a minister, evangelist, or Christian teacher, an essential question you need to ask is how much of your ministry is devoted to healing sicknesses of the body and mind? The scriptural evidence indicates that healing was a major focus of Jesus's ministry. As Jesus traveled from town to town, the healing needs of the world were presented to him in many very dramatic ways. No matter what Jesus's agenda may have been, he was always willing to heal any sick person who crossed his path. Jesus was always willing to change his schedule so that he could fulfill a healing need or request.

Let me tell you a story. In the early history of medicine, there was a time when science knew very little about the spread of germs and their relationship to sickness. When a knowledgeable physician suggested that something as simple as washing your hands and setting some basic standards of cleanliness would cut down on the spread of deadly infections, he was scorned. Nevertheless, he washed his hands and practiced good hygiene; low and behold, he achieved a better result. Today the washing of hands is seen as the first line of defense in retarding infections in the sick and the spread of infectious diseases.

Thus, the proof in a simple idea was in the doing. The challenge to Christians and to the church is not to reject the thesis of this book and my suggestions out-of-hand. Read this book and give these ideas some serious consideration. Examine the following ideas and suggestions and determine if there is some possible merit to what I am saying. Your challenge as a pastor or church leader is to incorporate a ministry of healing into your church ministry or into your Christian life. Repent, change your ideological or doctrinal thinking, and elevate healing to its proper place in your church. To determine the extent of the ideological changes that should be made, do the following:

1. Determine whether there is a basic ideological conflict between God as Jesus defines him and the God of the Old Testament.

2. In your church, discuss the ideas in this book in terms of what Jesus taught and the theological beliefs and practices in the Apostles' Doctrine, and determine the impact of these differences on faith, belief, and unbelief.

3. Decide if the theological basis for what I am suggesting about the confusion created by these opposite versions of God is true and biblically sound. If you find scriptural support for the veracity of my basic thesis, go to step four.

4. Develop a separate healing ministry with no other purpose than to heal. Be amazed that the kingdom of God, with all of its love, power, and light, will manifest in such a way that it will illuminate your life, church, and community so much that everyone and everything will be changed forever.

To develop a separate healing ministry, simply dedicate one of your monthly services specifically to healing. Make an announcement to the congregation and the community that the third Saturday, for example, will be a day of healing, and everyone in need of healing should come expecting a miracle. *Then in the service use the power of your persuasiveness to create an atmosphere of faith and power to dispel unbelief and inspire sufficient faith that healing in the name of Jesus can and will occur. Make of your sanctuary a "pool of Bethesda" where the "Spirit of God" is manifesting with such power that everyone can feel it and healing will flow like a mighty river. Sicknesses and diseases will be healed. When you do this, your ministry will be changed forever.*

I want to challenge every Christian teacher and leader who reads this book to reexamine the scriptures and decide if there is the remotest possibility that there may be some truth in what I have said. Moreover, should my basic premises that miracles of healing were essential elements of Jesus's ministry and that his expectations were that we should be doing the greater works of healing be validated scripturally, then develop a separate healing ministry based on the recommendations I have made. You will be astounded at the outcome!

I will end this brief monologue with a scripture that has sustained me through many trials and tribulations. Jesus said, "These things I have spoken unto you, that in me ye might have peace. In the world ye shall have tribulation: but be of good cheer; I have overcome the world" (John 16:33). I believe that the information in this book will be useful to you in developing a healing ministry in your church. Furthermore, if we are successful in developing reliable healing ministries in our churches, much fear will be eliminated from the world. We will then have a greater measure of the peace that Jesus left for us.

Now may the peace of God and the fellowship of the Holy Ghost rest and abide with each of you forever. Amen.

Further Reading

The following books have provided ideas, information, and inspiration that have been essential ingredients in the formulation of this book:

A Course in Miracles. Tiburon, CA: Foundation for Inner Peace, 1975.

Achtemeir, Paul, editor. *Harper's Bible Dictionary.* San Francisco, CA: Harper & Row, 1946.

Anonymous. *Christ in You.* Marina del Rey, CA: DeVorss & Company, 1910.

Cruden, Alexander. *Cruden's Complete Concordance.* Grand Rapids, MI: Zondervan, 1967.

Huber, Robert V., project editor. *The Bible Through the Ages.* Pleasantville, NY: U.S. General Books, Readers Digest, 1996.

Manchester, William. *A World Lit Only by Fire: The Medieval Mind and the Renaissance—Portrait of an Age.* Washington, DC: Library of Congress, 1992.

Cornerstone Bible Publishers. *The Master Study Bible.* Nashville, TN, 2001.

978-0-595-36680-4

0-595-36680-5

CPSIA information can be obtained
at www.ICGtesting.com
Printed in the USA
FSHW011333230221
78873FS